Verbalising the Visual
Translating art and design into words

Michael Clarke

For my many students

An AVA Book

Published by
AVA Publishing SA
Rue des Fontenailles 16
Case Postale
1000 Lausanne 6
Switzerland
Tel: +41 786 005 109
Email: enquiries@avabooks.ch

Distributed by
ex-North America
Thames & Hudson
181a High Holborn
London WC1V 7QX
United Kingdom
Tel: +44 20 7845 5000
Fax: +44 20 7845 5055
Email: sales@thameshudson.co.uk
www.thamesandhudson.com

Distributed by
in the USA & Canada
Watson-Guptill Publications
770 Broadway
New York, New York 10003
USA
Fax: 1-646-654-5487
Email: info@watsonguptill.com
www.watsonguptill.com

English Language Support Office
AVA Publishing (UK) Ltd.
Tel: +44 1903 204 455
Email: enquiries@avabooks.co.uk

Design
Malcolm Southward

Production
AVA Book Production Pte. Ltd.,
Singapore
Tel: +65 6334 8173
Fax: +65 6259 9830
Email: production@avabooks.com.sg

Index courtesy of Indexing
Specialist (UK) Ltd.

ISBN 2-940373-01-9
and 978-2-940373-01-7

10 9 8 7 6 5 4 3 2 1

Verbalising the Visual
Translating art and design into words

Michael Clarke

 Academia
the environment of learning

Contents

Contents

How to get the most out of this book

This book is structured in two parts, chapters one, two and three adopt a theoretical approach and explore the ways in which language is used to describe, analyse and critically evaluate art and design.

Chapters four, five and six demonstrate the application of the theory in the practical contexts of producing assignments, essays, reports and reviews and in the conducting of interviews, oral presentations, peer-group discussions and critical evaluations.

Chapter openers
Each chapter opens with a breaker spread that lists the section title and all associated units. Each chapter is colour coded to help aid navigation throughout the book.

Unit introduction
Each chapter unit is introduced in isolation, and outlines the key principles that will be explored.

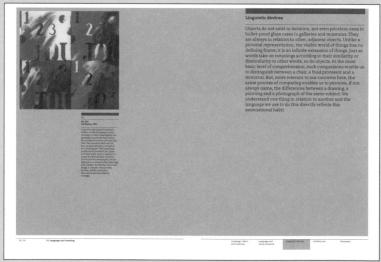

Captions
Captions help bring principles under discussion in the body text to life via examples of third party and author analysis of the images.

Chapter activities
Each of the three theoretical chapters contains an exercise that will help you better consider and begin to apply the concepts under discussion.

Chapter summaries
Every chapter is concluded with a summary of 10 key points.

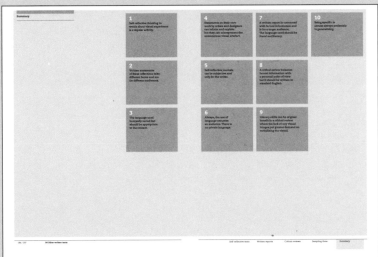

Chapter samplings
Each of the three practical chapters contains a sampling piece that will help you better consider and begin to apply the concepts under discussion.

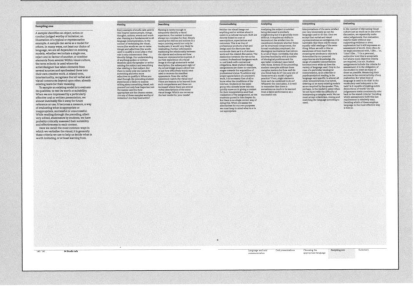

Introduction

Translating a visual experience into a verbal statement, spoken or written, is far from easy. Yet students of almost any of the expanding subjects within visual culture are expected, above and beyond their technical and creative abilities in their chosen discipline, to have the necessary skills to do so. Much like translating or interpreting any one written or spoken language into another, these skills can be learned, but they must first be identified, examined and evaluated so that an appropriate choice can be made from the available options to suit the specific requirements of a particular visual experience and its verbalisation. This book is specifically addressed to those students seeking guidance in acquiring these necessary skills.

Across all the various specialist courses in the practice of visual culture and the assignments set within each specialist area, students quickly find themselves confronted with the need to relate verbal and visual communication. Words and visual imagery may have more obvious proximity in subject areas such as film or graphic design. However, in the research, design development, realisation and evaluation of an art or design practical assignment, or the research, processing, presentation and assessment of an essay, report or critical review, an ability to verbalise the visual is essential. Acquiring and developing the necessary skills is imperative.

Visual culture

Visual culture is itself not easy to define. Superficially, it can suggest all visual phenomena, natural or cultural, but in the context of academic disciplines and expectations, it is most often restricted to culture; the visible artefacts and manifestations that we humans have brought into the world. For the purposes of this book, it embraces in its awareness, if not always in its direct verbal or visual references, those now very familiar areas of specialist study such as advertising, architecture, the fine arts, fashion, film, graphics, product design and photography.

This book also explores cultural and sub-cultural differences, questions of personal and collective identity, and the specific vocabularies and concepts particular to these groups. For example, the word 'bias' is, in its most general usage and most often within the context of art and design, used pejoratively to identify a prejudiced position or one that departs from standard norms of judgement. However, within the context of fashion, a garment described as being cut on the 'bias' neutrally describes cutting obliquely across the warp of the fabric. Language can never be taken at face value. Its interpretation and meaning are always very specific to the context in which it is used.

Despite the many problematic issues to do with verbalising the visual, this book is not prescriptive. It is not a 'how to' guide that, either explicitly or implicitly, claims any authority to instruct how one should speak, write or interpret statements about visual culture, although it will identify and examine all of these aspects. This book's overall approach is interrogative: asking questions rather than presuming any one answer and evaluating the options available rather than prescribing any one of them. There are no absolute techniques for verbalising the visual, only appropriate ones.

The book's structure divides into two roughly equal parts. The first three chapters examine respectively: the unstable relation between words, objects and meanings; the formal language used by professionals in art and design history, theory and related subjects; and the more informal, even colloquial language used by journalists and sub-cultural groups. The last three chapters are entirely focused on how practising students of art and design verbalise the visual; in oral discussions, presentations and interviews; in the context of the formal, written essay; and in a variety of other written contexts.

The two halves are meant to be reciprocal. Both parts include deconstructed examples of formal, academic, and informal, colloquial use of language but there is no intention to present the largely professional use of language examined in the first half as an exemplary model. Readers of this book are just as likely to benefit from the student examples used in the second half as the professional ones used in the first. Identifying and evaluating the different examples in order to make appropriate, effective statements of one's own is the primary concern.

01

Woodcut, Sasa Marinkov, 1988

Look carefully at this image. Restricting yourself to no more than two minutes and without hesitation or repetition, respond to the following:

1 Identify the subject
2 Describe the image
3 Say what you think it means
4 Without showing the picture, ask your friends what they imagine to be the image from your description
5 Show them the image so that you can test your abilities to verbalise the visual

01 Language and meaning

01

Language
and meaning

02

Language Is Not Transparent
Mel Bochner, 1970

Chalked onto a patch of dark paint like a piece of graffiti, the statement reminds us that words have no fixed relationship to the things they name, but are arbitrary.

01 Language and meaning

Language, object and meaning

Language is not transparent. Words cannot be compared to the panes of glass in a window, which allow us to directly connect with the things on the other side, although in ordinary speech and writing they may appear to be so. Even those well aware of the unstable relationship between words, objects and meanings will, for the most part, accept the conventional practices and assumptions of common language usage if only to achieve a reasonable level of communication.

Language, object
and meaning

Language and
visual artefacts

Linguistic devices

Activity one

Summary

Duality

The names we assign to things are not naturally given, as anyone living in a multilingual society will quickly become aware. However many recognisable characteristics the Italian, Spanish or French languages may have acquired from their shared origins in Latin, their vocabularies are not the same. The differences between languages further increase when the radius expands outwards from the Mediterranean to embrace Russian, Japanese or Arabic languages that all use other scripts. Language is always specific to a particular language culture and the words that are used are culturally determined.

Let us take the English word 'dog'. Ordinarily, both when we speak and write, we use the word as if it was inseparable from the creature it names. Yet there is nothing dog-like about the sound or the written (or printed) nature of the word. The relationship between the animal and the name we give it is arbitrary, as the variety of names used to represent a dog in other languages makes clear. If there were a natural relationship between an object and the word used to represent it, all languages would be the same. A word is not the union of an object and a name, but the union of the concept of an object and the word that represents it. The word 'dog' does not securely attach itself to any member of the species but to the idea of 'dogness'. The animal has escaped!

Ferdinand de Saussure

An awareness of the instability between words, objects and meanings is not new: it goes back at least as far as the ancient Greeks (this may be different for other language cultures). Our modern awareness of this instability begins with Ferdinand de Saussure (1857–1913), a Swiss linguist whose ideas laid the foundation for many of the significant developments in linguistics in the 20th century. Saussure's linguistics differed decisively from that of his contemporaries and predecessors. He adopted a synchronical (language in any one place and time), rather than a diachronical (language in one place but how it develops over time) analysis of language. It is what a language is rather than what it has become that formed the focus of Saussure's attention.

For Saussure, what made a word intelligible was not its connection to some essence, but its difference from another word in the same language system. As we have already seen, the words we use to name things are arbitrary. It is the difference between the spoken or written word 'dog' and other words, such as 'dock', 'doll', 'dolt', or 'dot', which lends significance. If you are speaking to a non-English person, in English or any other language, it is that much more important to pronounce the sounds clearly in order to be understood. As with sounds, so with ideas or concepts. Different languages inevitably produce different concepts. Members of one language group think and speak differently from those of another.

The still highly influential *Course in General Linguistics* (English translation 1974) was compiled from notes made by Saussure's students and although not easily summarised the following comes very near to a consensus:

'Language, Saussure says, is always organised in a specific way. It is a system, or a structure, where any individual element is meaningless outside the confines of that structure. In a strong and persistent passage in the Course, Saussure says: "in language (*langue*) there are only differences"…. The point is not only that value, or significance, is established through the relation between one term and another in the language system… but that the very terms of the system itself are the product of difference: there are no positive terms prior to the system…. Of equal importance for grasping the distinctiveness of Saussure's theory is the principle that language is a system of signs, and that each sign is composed of two parts: a signifier (*signifiant*) (word or sound-pattern), and a signified (*signifié*) (concept).'

John Lechte, *Fifty Key Contemporary Thinkers: From Structuralism to Postmodernity*, Routledge, 1994.

Dog
English

Hund
German / Swedish

Japanese

Собака
Russian

Arabic

03

Dog

For English-speaking readers and listeners, the German word 'hund' has a 't' sound at the end, but the same word in Swedish ends with a sound like the English 'd'. In Russian the word sounds like 'sabaka'; in Japanese the word sounds like 'inu'; in Arabic, the word sounds like 'kelb'. Neither visually nor aurally do any of these resemble a dog.

Hermeneutics

If languages are autonomous and without a fixed relation to material or abstract reality, it follows that the interpretation and understanding of any language statement cannot be fixed either. This is crucial in anything spoken or written about visual culture and it has radically influenced much major writing on art and design history, theory and criticism over the last half century.

One very significant outcome of this influence, one that is particularly important for the concerns of this book, is the enormous shift of emphasis from the author of a text to the reader. The effect of Saussure's analysis of language is to reduce the authority of the writer or speaker and increase the role of the reader or listener. Hermeneutics may be described as the development and study of theories of the interpretation and understanding of texts. Meaning becomes as much dependent upon the interpretations of the reader/listener as the intentions of the writer/speaker.

But in contemporary theory, the word text is used to identify not only written or printed matter but also any other kind of representation, including visual artefacts. In her 1969 essay 'Semiotike', Julia Kristeva persuasively argued that all texts are enmeshed in complex relationships with other existing texts in the same language/literary/visual culture. Thus the term *intertextuality* with its implications of an infinite extension of possible meanings.

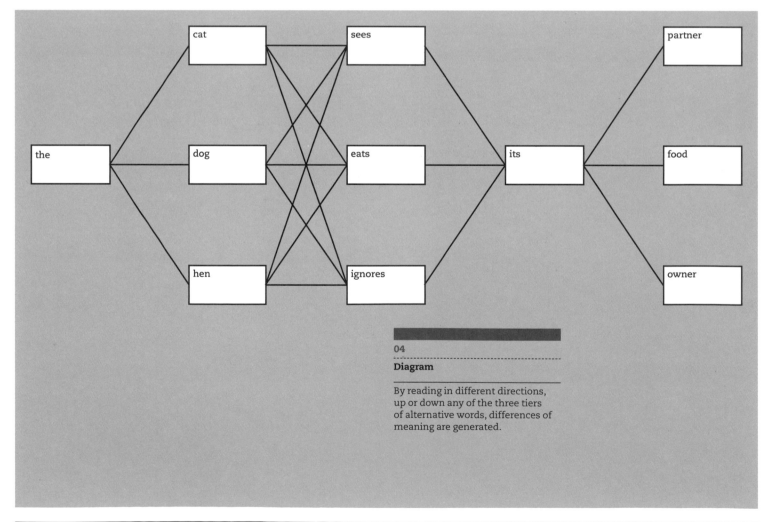

04

Diagram

By reading in different directions, up or down any of the three tiers of alternative words, differences of meaning are generated.

Barthes and Myth

Saussure's conviction was that language is a structure, a symbolic system of signs with each sign made up of two parts. A *sign* is not the combination of a name and a thing. It is the combination of a signifier, the sound of the word 'dog', and of the signified, in this instance the concept 'canine' or 'dogness'. It is through the operations of this symbolic system that the one thing can signify another and meaning becomes possible.

Roland Barthes was a French literary critic, social theorist, philosopher, and semiologist. His work extended over many fields and he influenced the development of schools of theory including structuralism, semiology and post-structuralism. Roland Barthes added a further component to the structure of language, that of myth. A reliable dictionary defines 'myth' as a widely held story or belief, especially an untrue or discredited popular one, and this is pertinent to Barthes' purpose.

In a series of very short essays written during the 1950s, all chosen from the objects and activities of popular culture, such as detergents or wrestling, Barthes conflates the traditional hierarchical distinctions between high and low culture by giving the same serious attention to commercial consumer items and the mass media as that normally reserved for the fine arts of painting, literature and music. Both individually and collectively, the essays convincingly show that even the most commonplace artefact or social event is rich in meanings, and the emerging discipline of *semiology*, or *semiotics* (the study of signs), provided a technique for revealing these.

Barthes' *Mythologies* (1957, translated into English 1972) decodes each subject, unmasking the concealed meaning behind the surface one. In the process, and especially in the much longer final essay, 'Myth Today', Barthes shows the extent to which myth relies upon unquestioned clichés and stereotypes, blurring the distinctions between the signifier and the signified in order to make verbal and visual representations appear as natural, given truths.

05

Wrestler

In his essay on wrestling, Barthes argues that all-in wrestling is a 'spectacle of excess'. He equates it with the grandiloquence of ancient classical theatre and its ritualised performances, which are already familiar to the regular audience before the action begins.

'Myth is a type of speech… Of course it is not any type of speech: language needs special conditions in order to become myth…myth is a system of communication, that is a message…Since myth is a type of speech, everything can be a myth provided that it is conveyed by a discourse…it is therefore by no means confined to oral speech. It can consist of modes of writing or of representations; not only of written discourse, but also photograph, cinema, reporting, sport, shows, publicity, all these can serve as a support of mythical speech.'

Roland Barthes, *Mythologies*, (original publication 1957, translated 1972) Vintage, 1993.

Foucault

Saussure also made a distinction between language (*la langue*) – the impersonal, collective, system of signs and their operations that make up the entire structure – and speech or writing (*parole*) – the specific ways in which individuals or groups use or inflect the language. It is this second distinction that allows us to identify the particular style or tone that distinguishes one writer from another as well as the specific language employed by members of a particular group, whether these be academics, lawyers, art and design historians and theorists, or any number of subcultural identities.

For French philosopher Michel Foucault, Saussure's *parole* becomes discourse, especially in its highly charged sense of an institutionalised way of speaking or writing, one that not only lays claim to authorship but also to authority. Where Barthes unmasked the concealed meaning behind the surface one, Foucault sought to expose the ways in which institutionalised groups with specific interests have used language to impose their values on others.

In *Les mots et les choses* (1966, translated as *The Order of Things*, 1970), Foucault advised that 'the world is covered with signs that must be deciphered, and those signs, which reveal resemblances and affinities, are themselves no more than forms of similitude. To know must therefore be to interpret: to find a way from the visible mark to that which is being said by it and which, without a mark, would be like unspoken speech, dormant within things.' Signs, whether verbal or visual, require interpretation if they are to convey any meaning at all, but their unavoidable ambiguities permit multiple readings. This becomes more complicated when the language used is that of a specialist discipline and the discourse it generates. If the discipline involves verbalising the visual, further complications arise.

Foucault wrote 'The relation of language to painting is an infinite relation. It is not that words are imperfect, or that, when confronted by the visible, they prove insuperably inadequate. Neither can be reduced to the other's terms: it is in vain that we say what we see; what we see never resides in what we say'. It is therefore inevitable that Foucault should have become interested in the work of the Belgian Surrealist painter, René Magritte, who, during the late 1920s, had been much preoccupied with verbal and visual semantics, the meanings we give to words and images, and especially, their association. Foucault's 1973 essay 'This Is Not a Pipe' addresses these problems by focusing attention on the complications that arise when we try to interpret Magritte's 1926 painting 'Ceci n'est pas une pipe': 'What misleads us is the inevitability of connecting the text to the drawing (as the demonstrative pronoun, the meaning of the word *pipe*, and the likeness of the image all invite us to do here) – and the impossibility of defining a perspective that would let us say that the assertion is true, false or contradictory.'

06

Ceci n'est pas une pipe
René Magritte, 1926

Both the representation of the pipe
and its textual denial are suspended
in an unidentifiable context, inviting
multiple speculation on the relation
between all the component parts:
physical, painted canvas; pictorial
and verbal elements; possible
interpretations and meanings.
Anyone seriously involved in
translating the visual into the verbal
must keep all these problematic
issues in mind.

07

**Flying Figure
Mary Spencer Watson, 1998**

The *Guardian* newspaper's obituary (18 March 2006) on Mary Spencer Watson stated that, 'it is as a carver of stone that she will be best remembered. She was always willing to experiment, letting the qualities of the stone – usually Purbeck – predominate and lead her imagination.'

Approaching the example above, this statement can help us see the sculpture in a wider context; but how would we describe and interpret what is particular to this piece? It is not only analytical skills that are required in order to identify what is distinct about the piece. We need language skills too.

Language and visual artefacts

We all constantly verbalise our visual experiences. A substantial part of our daily conversation with others is taken up with our need to give them some idea or impression of the people, things, places or events that we witnessed but they may not have seen. The frequently voiced claim that we live in a culture dominated by visual communication, advertising, film, television or the Net may be true but this has not diminished our need to articulate in words our response to this overwhelming visual culture. For students of art and design practice, it is a necessity. But how do we do this?

10

Apartment interior, Paris
Joseph Dirand, 2005

'Victor Baltard's massive 19th-century steel-and-stone construction remains precisely where it has always been, down on Boulevard Malesherbes, over a mile away on the other side of the Seine. The apartment plays host only to its dematerialised essence, a reflection trapped with obliging geometrical exactitude in a black mirrored wall recess....This is an ethereal space.'

Robert Shore, 'Blanc Expression', *The World of Interiors*, March 2006

08

Amiriya palace, Yemen
interior dome, 1504

'The tempera painting is extraordinary, the jewel of the Amiriya. There are rich reds, blues, greens and oranges, neat geometrical patterns and ornate floral designs.'

Rory McCarthy, *Guardian Weekend*, 11 March 2006

09

Eltham palace, London
interior, 1930s

'Though the palace is often cited as one of London's art deco gems, influences include Venetian palaces, classical temples, Parisian salons and Swedish modernism.'

Jessica Cargill Thompson, *Time Out*, London, 8–15 March 2006

If we consider the descriptions of these three interiors we might conclude that, although the Amiriya text begins with a value judgement ('extraordinary...etc.) and the Eltham Palace text with a critical one (Though often cited as...etc.), the former keeps very close to the visible evidence ('there are rich reds, blues, greens and oranges') while the latter adopts an analytical position ('influences include Venetian palaces, classical temples').

Both are very different from the Robert Shore text, which uses very suggestive language ('dematerialised essence', 'an ethereal space') to conjure up the experience of being in a very specific ambience. The position here is largely rhetorical, seeking to persuade us to accept a particular response, with or without any other evidence. Had there not been several photographic images accompanying the text, the reader could have had difficulty visualising the apartment and its borrowed views.

Naming

Naming is a fundamental activity of language. Try speaking or writing about a photograph, an illustration, an advertisement, an interior, or any visual image without identifying the objects, and the central role of naming becomes very evident, especially when we are entirely dependent upon the words to convey the visual appearance of something. Naming goes beyond the single noun we give to specific objects, as in 'dog'. It includes the names we use to identify different categories of things, as in still-life, product design, sculpture or photography.

Reaching out still further, it includes naming works of fine art. In any gallery, museum, temporary public or commercial exhibition, it isn't only the name of the artist or designer that viewers are seeking when they lean forward to read the little card on the wall. It is the title too. This alone indicates just how closely related are the visual and the verbal, even if the title turns out to be the paradoxical, 'this is not a pipe', or enigmatic, 'untitled'.

Describing

Describing our visual experiences is, perhaps, the most familiar practice and often involves a very delicate balance of interests. In ordinary conversation, this might be a highly subjective, emotionally or ideologically charged account revealing as much about the speaker as the subject of attention. Or it might be an impersonal, dispassionate account, one revealing the speaker's concern to be as objectively descriptive as possible. Neither is necessarily better than the other. If asked what were our responses to a specific work, exhibition, style or movement, the context of the request would help decide what manner of response was appropriate.

The key factor here is the known or expected audience. Talking to close friends with similar interests who share the same subcultural vocabulary and concepts as we do is easiest but what is being said or written in such circumstances may convey only limited or different meaning to others outside the subcultural group. A parallel exists among readers of specialist magazines and journals. They, too, are familiar with a particular kind of language to the point where many are sensitive to every allusion the specialist language contains, but this does not extend beyond the specialist audience.

There is a reciprocal factor involved. We are all in varying degrees aware of the distinctions between one kind of language and another, even to identifying the specific language used (Saussure's *parole*) within a specific social group. In Western cultures, this is easily done with legal and medical language but it is almost as easily done with academic language. Within the context of visual culture, the variety of descriptive language employed is immense. Classifying the language used is inevitably to associate it with the social and cultural class that uses such language. Descriptive language is never without these social and cultural connections, however indirectly they may be voiced.

11

Interior of the Tuschinski Cinema, Amsterdam
Pieter den Besten and Jaap Gidding
1918–21

'Superficially Gidding's dramatic and highly colourful designs have much in common with the decorative ethos of contemporary French decorative arts and the glitz of 1920s Hollywood film sets. However, the expressive possibilities afforded by the cinema's unified external and ornamental decorative schemes also had more in common with the expressive work of the Amsterdam School, a progressive strand of Dutch design opposed to the greater commitment to a modernist machine age aesthetic of contemporary De Stijl architects and designers.'

Jonathan M. Woodham, *Twentieth-century Design*, Oxford Paperbacks, 1997

Whenever anyone dissects or deconstructs an object into any set of constituent elements, they are engaging in analysis. Woodham's text breaks down the overall appearance of the interior into several stylistic influences, not just that of Art Deco. The text takes this approach further, edging towards comparisons and contrasts.

12

Dashboard for the Cadillac
Harley Earl, 1954

'At a time when science fiction and the beginnings of space travel had captured the imaginations of the general public, the large chrome-plated dials and controls arranged in the form of a cockpit gave the owner the illusion of being in control of sophisticated technology.'

Jonathan M. Woodham, 'Ornament and Industrial Design' in Jocelyn de Noblet (Ed.) *Industrial Design: Reflection of a Century*, Flammarion, 1993

The Cadillac dashboard is now more than half a century old and from a period when motorcar design in the USA was very different from that in other parts of the world. Few readers today will have any first-hand experience of this or similar dashboards. Woodham's accompanying text, by making connections between a collective enthusiasm for science fiction, aviation and the consumer's illusory sense of being in technical control, goes some way to reconstructing the particular context of the dashboard's design and meaning.

Contextualising

Identifying the context of the object of attention is to locate it in a particular time and place. Because all artefacts are products of specific conditions, social, economic, technical, cultural, both the character of the object and how it was understood at the time are determined by these factors. To include information of this kind in a commentary is to enlighten the reader or listener and this can be especially useful when the object is from an earlier time, another place, or both.

Very few if any readers of books, journals, magazines or newspapers are informed about the historical and social context of all the world's cultures. For example, a Westerner's enthusiasm for Japanese 18th- and 19th-century prints does not necessarily include an awareness of the context in which these were designed, produced, used and understood, yet these factors, once understood, contribute to a fuller understanding and appreciation, reaching beyond the Westerner's primary, aesthetic response. Contextualising Japanese prints liberates us from our own Western assumptions and expectations, as it does for all other artefacts from different cultural contexts.

But this is true, also, even for the culture in which we were born and reared. For example, consider how many Europeans might be able to locate Michelangelo's Sistine Chapel within the context of early 16th-century Italy. How different would our interpretations of any of the images reproduced here be if they were not given a cultural context?

Analysing

Another way in which we are often made aware of significant aspects of an artefact, either unnoticed or unknown to us, is through analysis. When practised by highly articulate people with detailed knowledge of any one or more ideological approaches, be it Marxist, psychoanalytical, semiological, or any other, this can become very complex, couched as such approaches always are in very specialised vocabulary.

Any analysis based upon a single ideological discipline has no claim to impartiality. However much any ideological discipline is able to reveal about an artefact, it is never, and never can be, conclusive. It is always a particular point of view. There are always alternative analyses of equal interest and validity. That is why any attempt to interpret a visual artefact or ensemble is always limited.

13

Mimic
Jeff Wall, 1982

'In the 80s, Wall thought his pictures should be about something. His 1982 Mimic, for instance, which looks like amazingly lucky street photography but was performed by actors in front of lights and a large-format camera, was "about" racism.'

Melissa Denes, *Guardian Weekend*, 15 October 2005

This photograph very quickly makes us aware just how complicated a matter it is to interpret even an apparently banal scene. Are all three figures together? Are the two men looking at each other? What significance do we attribute to the eyes of the man on the left or the hand gesture of the one on the right? Presented with the picture alone, we must decide. Given a title influences our response. Reading commentaries in which we are told that the scene 'was performed by actors' and 'was "about" racism' unavoidably changes our interpretation.

14

Palm House, Kew Gardens, London
Richard Turner and
Decimus Burton, 1844–1848

'Kew's Palm House is possibly the world's greatest surviving Victorian building, an awe-inspiring structure somewhere between a train station and a giant blancmange mould; it captures both the engineering brilliance and the exuberant vanity of its era.'

Steve Rose, 'Now You See It', *Guardian*, 6 March 2006

15

Musician,
Mary Spencer Watson, 1954–55

'Mary Spencer Watson…is still little known and remarkably undervalued. This may be due, in part, to the fact that her work, though resolutely modern, has less in common with today's celebrity conceptualists than with the medieval carvers and worker-craftsmen whose cathedral carvings she so greatly admired.'

Brian Morley, Mary Spencer Watson Obituary, *Guardian*, 18 March 2006

Interpreting

All the above activities, named on the previous pages (describing, contextualising or analysing), can be employed in an interpretation. An interpretation can be very short or very long. It is never, however, simple. In any attempt to explain the meaning or significance of an artefact, complex issues concerning perception, knowledge, expectation, referencing and evaluation arise. As we have seen at the beginning of this chapter, any verbal statement, written or spoken, needs in turn to be interpreted by the reader or listener. Unlike the numbers in pure mathematics, words have no fixed value and cannot claim any single meaning. During this process of double interpretation, differences of opinion and, sometimes, open disagreement can easily arise.

It is sometimes thought that interpreting images of functional artefacts, such as a food processor or digital camera, is easier than interpreting works of fine art, be they painted, sculpted, photographed or otherwise. At least the utilitarian, functional dimensions of the artefacts might provide a common basis for understanding. Without any comparable basis in the practical, fine art artefacts are judged to be far less contained.

Evaluating

Practising students of the visual arts very early in the first weeks of their study become involved in the interim evaluation of art or design projects. This can be a one-to-one conversation with a tutor but it is very often a group activity in which the progress of each individual's project is discussed. It is during these group sessions that students quickly become aware how easily the interpretation of their work overlaps with an appraisal of it.

To critically evaluate an artefact is to engage in estimating the amount of worth we give to one or more aspects of it and it most typically employs several sets of *binary* opposites easily recognised in the words used to pass judgement: accessible, inaccessible; convincing, unconvincing; successful, unsuccessful; better, worse; major, minor; good, bad. To use any one of the words in these equations is to pass judgement; to use more than one is to adopt a much more clearly identifiable, overall evaluation. Keeping in mind the binary opposite of any of the above or other binary terms is a very useful way of estimating the position of the speaker or writer.

Evaluative statements can be as unassertive as the phrase 'still little known and remarkably undervalued' in the obituary of Mary Spencer Watson, or, despite the qualifying 'possibly' as challenging as the claim that the Kew Gardens Palm House is 'the world's greatest surviving Victorian building'. Identifying the context in which these statements were made can help us to better understand the intended meaning. However, ultimately we must set all such statements beside their contraries to more fully appreciate their claims.

16

Jou-Jou
J M Clarke, 1973

Linguistic and visual devices are
evident in this lithographic print.
Numbers in their unambiguity are
generally considered denotatory,
but combined as here with circular
discs like counters, each and all
four squares become a metaphor
for a board game. This is perhaps
confirmed in the word 'jou' (*jouer*
in French is the verb to play) but it
is also the first syllable of *journal*
(the French for newspaper), which
appears in so many Cubist paintings
and collages. Via number, word and
image, a complex relationship
between simile, metaphor,
denotation and connotation
emerges.

Linguistic devices

Objects do not exist in isolation, not even priceless ones in bullet-proof glass cases in galleries and museums. They are always in relation to other, adjacent objects. Unlike a pictorial representation, the visible world of things has no defining frame, it is an infinite extension of things. Just as words take on meanings according to their similarity or dissimilarity to other words, so do objects. At the most basic level of comprehension, such comparisons enable us to distinguish between a chair, a food processor and a motorcar. But, more relevant to our concerns here, the same process of comparing enables us to perceive, if not always name, the differences between a drawing, a painting and a photograph of the same subject. We understand one thing in relation to another and the language we use to do this directly reflects this associational habit.

17

Zambia
Nathalie du Pasquier, 1982

'In a confused age when a sense of
history and popular culture meet,
Memphis can perhaps be described
as the ultimate "fruit salad"....
Memphis objects seem to be almost
edible, painted in food colours,
with references to cassata and
tutti-frutti. Nathalie du Pasquier's
fabrics have been compared to
sweet wrappers.'

Michael Collins, *Towards Postmodernism: Design Since 1851*, British
Museum Press (second revised
edition), 1994

Nathalie du Pasquier's textiles,
designed when she was actively
engaged with the Milan-based
agency, Memphis, can and have
been seen to epitomise that agency's
pleasure in often highly eclectic,
usually very synthetic, surface
decoration. In his commentary on
these characteristics, Michael
Collins mixes simile and metaphor
with highly suggestive, expanding
effect ('the ultimate fruit salad'
metaphor extending via 'almost
edible' to 'references to cassata and
tutti-frutti'), the reference to sweet
wrappers sending out ripples of
pleasurable associations.

Simile

Recognising a likeness between things is a
common experience and ubiquitous in
speaking or writing about visual culture. When
we do this, we are using a simile. The impact of
a first encounter with the original of an
admired work of art is often expressed by the
statement, 'It was like opening my eyes for the
first time.' Likening the work of one artist or
designer to another is, likewise, a regular
practice in describing and interpreting visual
artefacts. So too is likening the form or
structure of an artefact to an otherwise
different model.

Similes are closely connected to any form of
the mimetic in which, through words, actions
or visual images, an attempt is made to
imitate the characteristics of a person, thing or
action. Simulation, therefore, is a primary aim
of all representations that seek to be the
equivalents of what they represent. Ever since
Aristotle, for whom the mimetic was a central
factor in his understanding of both the
temporal and spatial arts, likening one thing
to another has retained its importance.

18

The Diva Is Dismissed,
Paula Scher, 1994

'Sans serif type runs in various
directions in contrasting scales,
fitted together like the pieces of
a puzzle. Scher's approach recalls
vernacular theatre posters and
tickets that carve the available
space into zones and then fill
them to the brim.'

Ellen Lupton, *Mixing Messages:
Contemporary Graphic Design in North
America*, Thames & Hudson, 1996

Lupton's suggestive language ('fitted
together like the pieces of a puzzle')
encourages the reader to pursue
closely related connections in the
expectation that by doing so they
will be enlightened, their
understanding and appreciation of
the work will be extended.

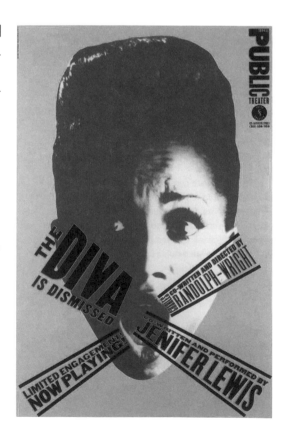

Metaphor

Our recognition of likeness between one thing and another can be so great that we see it as analogous, a proximity so close that it is taken to be an equivalent, one thing standing for another. When we judge someone to be 'blind' because they cannot recognise the merits of an artist or designer admired by us, we are not speaking or writing literally, in the sense that they cannot physically see, but metaphorically, in the sense that it is as if they cannot see. The same is true when a visual image is said to be 'exploding with energy' or 'reticent to the point of silence'. Neither 'exploding' nor 'silence' are characteristics one can reasonably attribute to a mute, static artefact unless, as is the usual case, they are meant to be understood as equivalents. Where a simile acknowledges that something is like another, a metaphor more confidently replaces the other.

Denotation

In order to distinguish one object from another, language enables us to name things. At this most basic level it enables us to designate an object (chair) or category of objects (furniture) at the least disputable level of understanding. This is the denotatory level of meaning.

Maintaining this denotatory level in any description, analysis or evaluation of a visual artefact requires enormous linguistic skill, a skill more frequently evident in the legal profession than that of art and design history, theory or criticism. For example, confronted with any visual representation of a dog, we might readily decide that it is a dog not a cat.

But is it only a dog? Given our awareness of the instability and flexibility of language or visual images, their openness to variable interpretation, naming or otherwise representing something rarely if ever is restricted to the denotative level of understanding. A dog is an animal, part of nature, man's best friend, and so on. The significance we attach to an object, or the name we give it, is restricted only by our own limitations of experience or knowledge. We are the interpreters.

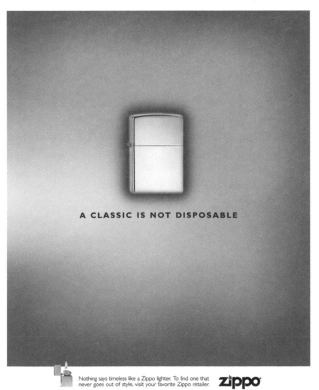

A CLASSIC IS NOT DISPOSABLE

Nothing says timeless like a Zippo lighter. To find one that never goes out of style, visit your favorite Zippo retailer. **zippo**

19

Zippo advertisement, 1932–62

Beyond the recognisable cigarette lighter there are suggestive elements such as the bright central flame, the diminishing light towards the edges of the image, and the statement, 'a classic is not disposable', which is a verbal attempt to persuade us into accepting the Zippo as an enduring design classic.

Connotation

Like the ripples from a pebble dropped in a pond, words and visual images always carry more possible meanings than their obvious surface ones. Only the most literal-minded person is unresponsive to the allusive, suggestive levels of an image. For professionals and students directly involved in the making and interpretation of visual images, an acute awareness of the connotative dimensions of the image is a vital element in their understanding and appreciation of visual culture.

Neither words, in whatever configuration or verbal category, nor visual images, in whatever medium or location, exist outside the context of other words and visual images. Understood in a generic sense, any text, verbal, visual, musical or whatever, is always produced and understood in the context of other existing texts, as Julia Kristeva and others have shown. This intertextuality, an infinite network of possible connections, is always capable of producing a diversity of equally valid interpretations. Likewise, every text is produced and received within a specific set of cultural conditions; social, economic, political, etc. No text ever quite escapes the characteristics that identify it with these cultural conditions. Together, these connotative dimensions of a text go way beyond the denotative level of significance.

20

Pinter vs the US
Daniel Pudles, 2005

A denotatory description of Daniel Pudles's illustration might identify little more than some red vertical bars capped with white stars on blue squares with a skull-like head and skeletal hand appearing from behind these elements. Yet, even out of its original context, few interpretations will fail to engage with the socio-political suggestions these elements encourage. The implication of something beyond what is expressly stated or represented is the connotative dimension to a visual image or text.

21

Bertolli advertisement, 2006

Commercial advertisements very often rely heavily on connotative imagery to achieve their effects. Although at the denotative level the Bertolli advertisement is a greengrocer's stall with vendor and customer, both the amount and variety of vegetables readily suggest a cornucopia, a large horn full to the brim with the fruits of the earth. The predominance of red, green and white in an image used to promote this particular brand easily connotes the Italian flag.

Sagatiba advertisement, 2006

There are connotations of national
identity in the Sagatiba
advertisement too and, like the
Bertolli, any interpretation of it
cannot fail to make the connections.
Although the young man is very
evidently in a room with a billiard
table, the way he is holding the
billiard stick suggests a crucifixion.
His face and hair identify him with
a very specific image, the colossal
sculpture of Cristo Redentor, Christ
the Redeemer, that stands on
Corcovad above Rio de Janeiro
in Brasil.

23

'Job' poster
Alfons Mucha, 1898

Interpreting Alfons Mucha's famous
'Job' poster prompts the use of all
the linguistic devices mentioned:
from the denotative brand name to
the connotations of the ensnaring
(metaphor), tentacle-like (simile)
hair, placing the abundant,
curvilinear hair within the Art
Nouveau style (contextualising)
and noting the recurrence of a
decorative version of 'Job' in
the wallpaper background and
brooch (analysing).

Activity one
The relationship between language and artefacts

This is an exercise that is designed to develop an awareness of the relationship between language and artefacts. Look at these three images and read the text that accompanies each.

Consider the relation between the text and the visual image in the following three examples.

1 Is the text primarily descriptive, informational, or interpretative?

2 Does the text add anything to your understanding of the image?

3 What kind of language is used?

24

Graveyard, Houses and Steel Mill, Bethlehem, Pennsylvania
Walker Evans, 1935

'In the context of Evans's images of America, this is both daunting and depressive. The houses to the right are archetypal Hopper, although the scene is overwhelmingly industrial and urban. The photograph is given substance by the white cross. This is very much an image that suggests the "death" of American culture and is a clear precursor of Frank's "The Americans"'.

Graham Clarke, *The Photograph: A Visual and Cultural History*, Oxford Paperbacks 1997

25

iMac computer
Apple, 1998

'The cabinet of Apple Computer's "iMac" was principally in the hands of Jonathan Ive (b.1967), Apple's head of design since 1996. He had studied industrial design in England before being introduced to Apple while working at Tangerine, a London design studio he co-founded in 1990. His first design as an Apple employee was the "Newton MessagePad 110" of 1992. Numerous other assignments followed including the "20th Anniversary Mackintosh" of 1993–96. Two levels below Steven Jobs who became the returning saviour of Apple in 1997, Ive vowed that Apple's next products would be "targeted to individuals rather than large unfocused groups…and be the most exciting and meaningful designs that Apple has ever delivered." The pledge was realized as the "iMac". Fanatical attention was paid to every minute aspect of the integrated body, the compatible keyboard, and the pill-box mouse – machinery intended to put households in touch with the World Wide Web. The translucent shell revealed a fuzzy picture of the powerful workings inside. Even the mouse's intestines could be seen. The tangle of wires found at the back end of previous beige-bodied computers was banished. The "iMac" was a far cry from Jobs's first born, the "Apple I" of 1975, and the formality of Hartmut Esslinger's "Apple SE" of 1987. A century later, the first electric typewriter, the Blickensderfer of 1901, had miraculously metamorphosed into the little "blue egg".'

Mel Byars with Arlette Barre-Despond, *100 Designs/100 Years: Innovative Designs of the 20th Century*, Diane Publishing Company, 2001

26

'Direction' cover design
Paul Rand, 1942

'Paul Rand designed a series of covers for the magazine *Direction* between 1938 and 1945. *Direction* was a cultural arts publication which occasionally dealt with world events. Rand demanded freedom in these designs and they exemplify the power of Rand's visual ingenuity at its best. This cover, from 1942, uses two powerful symbols to communicate a powerful message in wartime America, namely that the eagle (the US) was claiming the rat (the Axis powers). The sketchy drawing technique used by Rand enhances the strength of the image'.

R. Roger Remington, *American Modernism: Graphic Design 1920 to 1960*, Yale University Press, 2003

1

Language is not transparent. The names we give to things are arbitrary.

2

The relation between word, object and meaning is unstable. Words acquire meaning in relation to other words, not things.

3

Identifying the historical and cultural context of an image is always revealing.

4

Analysing a visual image directs attention to its constituent elements and how they interact.

7

We understand one thing in relation to another. Identifying a likeness between things, as in a simile, is a common example of associational thinking.

10

What the various elements in a visual image suggest or connote are essential in the thinking of both the creator and interpreter of images.

5

Interpreting a visual image involves a complete engagement with all its elements and possible meanings. It is a complex process and never conclusive.

8

Representing one thing as equivalent to another, as in a metaphor, is a further example of associational thinking.

6

Evaluating a visual image is equally complex with many factors contributing to the amount of value we apportion to one or more of its aspects.

9

The denotatory level of naming and describing stays as close as possible to the visibly evident, least disputable aspects of an image.

02

Formal language: the academic disciplines of art and design

27

The Pantheon, Rome
AD 118–125

Judged a masterpiece by
architectural historians and critics,
the Pantheon is a key work in the
classical canon, the pedimented and
colonnaded portico leading into a
cylindrical domed hall. Like
comparable works of sculpture and
painting, it has served as an
influential model for many
successive architects trained in the
academic tradition. The Latin
inscription, identifying Agrippa as
the builder, reminds us that it is
also from the languages of the
ancient classical world that the
Western tradition of academic
writing is derived.

Academic language

Ekphrasis, the word that most accurately identifies the activity of describing or explaining artefacts, is of ancient Greek origin, and like so many other words used in traditional and more recent art history, theory and criticism, it is alien to even most Western students. All academic disciplines have their own specialised vocabulary and concepts, inherited through centuries of professional practice, but in fulfilling the need for a precise language that minimises the possibility of unintended meanings, academic disciplines erect linguistic barriers that accidentally or intentionally exclude all but the initiated. The authority conceded to professional institutions often relies upon an exclusive language. How many people anywhere in the world know the medical or legal terms used by the professionals within these disciplines? However, as soon as the specialist language of any professional discipline is decoded, demythologised, the barrier is breached. Then the necessary use of specialist language is separated from the unnecessary jargon and most students begin to find themselves empowered, no longer excluded from professional discourse.

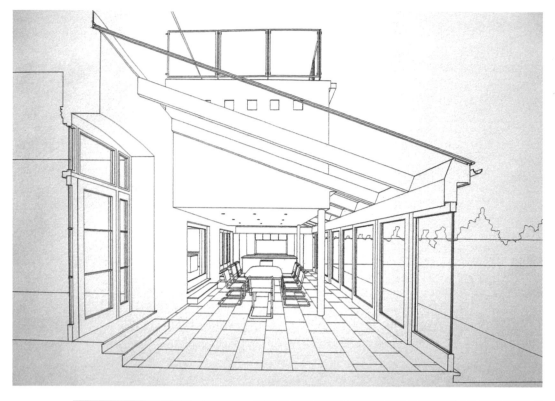

**Conservatory perspective,
Balham Park Road, London
Michael Jones, 1999**

The mathematical basis of linear perspective represents the world as rationally ordered. It is a regular and regulating system ideally suited to presentation drawings, as here. The proportions and spatial dimensions of the proposed conservatory and its furnishing are clearly represented.

29

**Virgin and child with
St Anne and St John
Leonardo da Vinci, c.1500**

Chiaroscuro and sfumato techniques are characteristic of Leonardo's mature work. The former persuasively represents the fall of light on the surfaces of objects. The latter recreates the softened, even unfocused appearance of objects under varying atmospheric effects.

The western canon

Western art history is often said to have begun with Giorgio Vasari (1511–74). Italian art and architecture, to which he both contributed and wrote about, perhaps inevitably became the central subject of interest to the first professional art historians in the late 19th and early 20th centuries. The title of Vasari's major book, *The Lives of The Most Excellent Italian Painters, Sculptors and Architects* (1550, enlarged 1568) suggests the priorities that were to be widely accepted and the vocabulary and concepts that sustained them. Almost all of these priorities are based upon hierarchical selection and judgement: the fine arts of painting, sculpture and architecture (the various crafts recognised only if their designers were a major artist); the master, always male and credited with unexplained genius; the *masterpiece*, defined as epitomising the highest, claimed virtues; the *canon*, the catalogue of masterpieces by masters said to exemplify the *Grand Tradition*.

An enduring technical vocabulary, itself frequently Italian and much of it still used in the studios of Western schools of art, architecture and design, has helped sustain the influence of the Italian Renaissance.

The innovations of linear and subsequently aerial perspective – in which receding parallel lines and planes are projected onto a flat surface with a common vanishing point and in which objects diminish in scale and clarity as they move away from the viewer – radicalised visual representation and are techniques still commonly used today. As are some additional techniques: contrapposto, in which the torsions of the body are set in contrary directions; chiaroscuro, the gradations of tone from light to dark; sfumato, a more subtle modulation of tone sufficient to suggest atmospheric effects.

A parallel technical vocabulary supported the description, analysis and evaluation of architecture, which had its own masters, masterpieces and canon. With its origins in ancient Greece and Rome, the classical language of architecture (albeit evolving) is the longest surviving tradition in the West (other cultures have their own different architectural traditions and conventions).

In the ancient temple, the orders, the distinct columns named after the regions of their origin, control not only the structure of the building but the building's proportions too. They are as important in architectural language as the verb is in verbal language. The spacing of each column was a vital concern. The Romans placed so much emphasis upon the intervals between the columns that they identified five standard types based on multiples of a column's diameter from the narrowest, pycnostyle, to the widest, araeostyle. Variations on these created visual rhythm, a parallel to that in speech or music. Such subtleties in the articulation of the elements of a building generated an equally subtle and discriminating specialist language, as in the three-part division of the entablature (the whole horizontal section between the column and the pediment) into the architrave, frieze and cornice. From the Roman Vitruvius to the Renaissance Serlio and beyond, this verbalising of the visual has helped establish the norms of classical architecture.

The western tradition

The term Renaissance or renascence (*rinascenza* or *rinascimento* in Italian) means rebirth, and what was being reborn here was the pagan, Western Classical Tradition, immediately recognisable in architecture and in stark contrast to the intervening Christian, Gothic visual culture of the cathedrals. From the outset, the Italian Renaissance was seen as progressive, every gain in knowledge or technique judged an improvement. The increasingly sophisticated achievement of verisimilitude (a true likeness) in painting and sculpture (albeit idealised) was proof of this. However many internal disagreements may have occurred over the subsequent centuries, Western academies of art and architecture accepted and promoted these ideals as universal values, supposedly applicable to any culture anywhere in the world, even into the early decades of modern art, architecture and design.

30

A seated nude male, turned to the right
Michelangelo Buonarotti, c.1504

Hatching and cross-hatching, the layering of short parallel lines, creates the tonal effects here; an alternative technique for modulating the fall of light across a surface. But the foreshortened presentation of the thighs and lower arm present a convincing, spatial image of the twisted body.

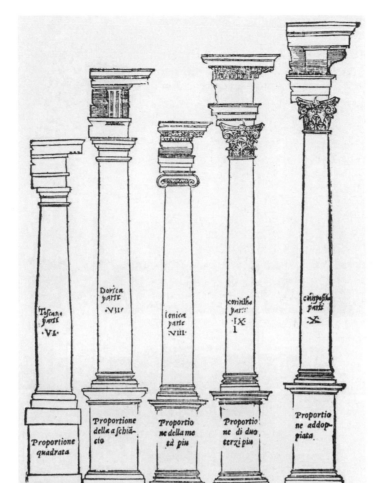

The five orders
Sebastiano Serlio, 1537

Central to Western classical architectural language were the Orders, five in all, their separate components rising from a base through the column to a capital and entablature. Three of the orders are named after the regions in Greece from which they were said to come, Doric, Ionic, Corinthian, and one a Composite of these. The fifth is, significantly, named Tuscan, the birthplace of Italian Renaissance art and architecture. Resting on this essentially post and beam structure (the technical term is trabiated), is the triangular-hipped roof with its elaborated end section, the pediment. The cupola, or drum and dome (the cylinder and its hemispherical conclusion) are a further extension of both the structural evolution of the classical language of architecture and its technical vocabulary.

Villa Rotonda
Andrea Palladio, 1550–51

The mathematical proportions, symmetry and lucid structure of this villa are clearly apparent. The balance between its use of pure, geometrical forms (cubes, cylinders, triangles, etc.) and refined, classical detailing in the columns, pediment, sculptures and elsewhere epitomised the architectural ideals of the High Renaissance.

Language across
the disciplines

Language and art
and design history

Language and art
and design theory

Language
and ideology

Activity two

Summary

The legacy

Today, the universalising system of Western, academic classicism may have been discredited (how can it be usefully applied to non-Western arts?) yet it has left a legacy, not least in our continuing habit of dividing the history of the visual arts into successive styles (for example, Baroque, Rococo or Neo-classical), movements (for example Mannerist, Romantic or Surrealist), dynasties (for example, Carolingian, Jacobean or Mughal) and, especially in the 20th century, the proliferation of 'isms' (Fauvism, Cubism or Constructivism for instance). More theoretically, some distinct approaches were developed and employed which, however much they may have been modified, revised or adapted, have contributed to contemporary modes of address.

The formalist position is one of these. Formalists emphasise direct contact with artefacts, their visible, physical attributes, such as line, shape, texture, colour and their formal relations, rather than the interpretation of subject, composition, historical and narrative possibilities or, least of all, social relations. Following the practice of Heinrich Wölfflin (1864–1945) a typical analysis of a painting would measure the linear against the painterly (the tightly drawn contour against the more loosely brushed), the use of open or closed forms (forms clearly enclosing an object or opening out to their surroundings), what is parallel with the surface and what is recessive (forms either complementary to or denying the two-dimensional nature of the drawn or painted plane), the rough and the smooth, and so on. This position prioritises an aesthetic response: one that comes through the senses, and discounts any other. The limited, formalist vocabulary initially raises questions about the limitations of the approach, but when successfully connected to a psychoanalytical interpretation, in which form itself is analysed, it can be revelatory.

33

Maharaja Rajansingh on an elephant Mughal Indian (Jhalai), 1820

The specialist language developed to verbally articulate one visual culture is rarely appropriate to another. The vocabulary and concepts associated with Western classicism cannot do justice to an image as different as this one in which linear perspective, chiaroscuro or contrapposto play no part.

Iconography, strictly speaking the study of images ('icon' is the ancient Greek equivalent of the Latin *imago*, meaning image), but in practice tracking their modifications, transformations and transpositions through different times and places, has had an equally durable influence. Following the practice of Erwin Panofsky (1892–1968), an iconographic analysis would refuse any division between form and content (outward visible appearance and any internalised meaning) acknowledging a connection between the visual arts and their cultural context even though this might depend upon a great deal of cultural and linguistic awareness. Iconography has links with post-Saussurian cultural analyses, especially semiology, the interpretation or decoding of verbal, visual or any other sign system.

Plurality

It is widely recognised today that there is no single history of visual culture as a whole. Universalising histories and theories of art, architecture and design, like those of visual culture in general, no longer have the support of a majority. Without a single history or theory there can be no single language to encompass all of the possibilities. Each specialised discipline whether of cultural context (such as Mayan, Hindu or Tang), category (fashion, industrial design or photography, for example), or ideology (for instance Marxist, psychoanalytical or semiological), generates its own vocabulary and concepts. A major problem for the student of contemporary history, theory and criticism of visual culture is the degree to which so many interpretations in any of these specialist disciplines draw upon an eclectic range of historical, theoretical, critical and linguistic practice.

34

Visvandatha temple
Khajuraho, India
10th–12th century

Beyond the use of upright walls, posts and beams, a very different architectural tradition is employed in this Hindu temple. It requires an equally different, specialist language from that used to verbalise the Western classical tradition.

Language across
the disciplines   Language and art
and design history   Language and art
and design theory   Language
and ideology   Activity two   Summary

02 Formal language: the academic disciplines of art and design Academic language

35

A stack of current books,
magazines and newspapers

Open the pages of any of the
publications reproduced in this
photograph and you will soon find
writing about the visual, whether
the visual be the lived experience of
private and public events or the
more deliberately constructed
artefacts of graphics, fashion,
industrial design, architecture or
any other product of visual culture.
The language used might be formal,
informal or an admixture but it
more than likely will include
historical, theoretical and critical
assumptions, whether consciously
or not.

Language across the disciplines

Another problem is how to distinguish between the history, theory and criticism of visual culture in a specific text. After only a brief survey of recent writing, it becomes difficult to conceive how any substantial statement on visual culture, spoken or written, could be made without there being an implicit, if not explicit, inclusion of all three. A typical statement such as, 'I think Picasso is the greatest artist of the 20th century', is explicit in its identification of historical period and its critical-evaluative judgement. It implicitly prioritises, on whatever theoretical basis, Western progressive art over any from elsewhere in the same century or even any more traditional, Western kind of painting or sculpture. Overlaps such as these are commonplace in writing about visual culture.

Complexities and contradictions

The balance between giving a progressive account of something (history), justifying an interpretation (theory) and evaluating the evidence (criticism) is variable from one author or book to another and rarely, if ever, declared.

The language used in titles and subtitles of books and essays can conceal as much as it reveals. Titles beginning 'The history of…' invariably fail to fulfil their all-embracing claim, least of all that of being the one and only, definitive account, which the use of the definite article 'the' leads one to expect. Titles beginning 'A History of…' avoid such extreme ambitions but the implication that this is only one possible point of view can be compromised and even contradicted by a text where the author too often assumes the position of uncontested authority.

It is the table of contents and ultimately the text itself that usually reveal most. Where the subject is very focused, the title, subtitle and table of contents are frequently accurate representations of the text that follows. This is most often the case with short essays.

General accounts, even of specific categories of visual culture such as painting, photography or interior design, are least likely to deliver what their titles and subtitles claim. Whether 'The' or 'A' history of art, books produced in the West are invariably written from a Western point of view, critically favour certain groups and individuals over others, without offering any theoretical basis for their exclusivity.

36

The Strand, London

Robert Venturi's preference for heterogeneity over homogeneity is stated below and illustrated here: 'Architects can no longer afford to be intimidated by the puritanical moral language of orthodox Modern architecture. I like elements which are hybrid, rather than "pure", compromising rather than "clean", distorted rather than "articulated"… I am for messy vitality over obvious unity. Is not Main Street almost all right?'

Robert Venturi, *Complexity and Contradiction in Architecture*, Museum of Modern Art, New York (second edition), 1977

Of the three authors quoted in this subsection, Robert Venturi is the most theoretical, his provocative thesis appropriately couched in the rhetorical language of binary oppositions. Robert Hughes' language is much more conversational, determined probably by the book's origin in a television series, his text mixing historical, theoretical and critical approaches in a single paragraph. Kenneth Frampton is, as the title of his book accurately states, critical, consistently comparing, contrasting and evaluating the architects and buildings he discusses. He is also explicit about his point of view.

'My *interpretative* stance has varied according to the subject under consideration. In some instances I have tried to show how a particular approach derives from *socio-economic* or *ideological* circumstances, while in others I have restricted myself to *formal analysis*.' (My italics). Kenneth Frampton, *Modern Architecture: A Critical History*, Thames & Hudson (revised third edition), 1992

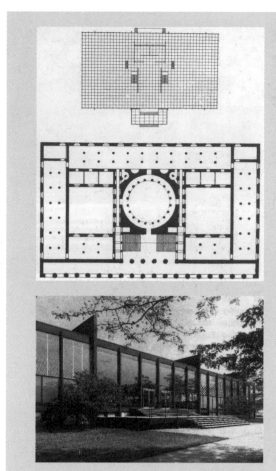

37b
....
Crown Hall, Illinois Institute of Technology, USA
Ludwig Mies van der Rohe, 1950–56

'Crown Hall…was a decisive return to the tradition of Schinkel and in particular to Schinkel's Altes Museum in Berlin, always admired by Mies. This Schinkelschuler type-form is generally evident as an organizing paradigm throughout Mies's work of the late 1960s…. Needless to say, the programme could not always be appropriately accommodated within such a simple paradigm. Thus, where the School of Social Services with its centralized library to the rear permitted a more or less direct transposition of the portico entry and rotunda of the Altes Mueseum, Crown Hall could but barely reflect these constituent elements and then only at the expense of the programme.'

Kenneth Frampton, *Modern Architecture: A Critical History*, Thames & Hudson (revised third edition), 1992

38
....
Red and blue chair
Gerrit Rietveld, 1918

'(Gerrit) Rietveld was a member of an idealist group in the Netherlands named De Stijl – "the style", suggesting a final consensus about form and function at the end of history, the ultimate style. Rietveld's "Rood Blaume Stoel" or "Red and Blue Chair", 1918, is considered a classic of its kind, and quite rightly. It so transcends ordinary functionalist discomfort that the only buttocks suited to it would need to be a cleft perfect solid. It is not furniture, but sculpture: a three-dimensional development of the two-dimensional pattern of grid and primary colours that formed the paintings of van Doesberg and Mondrian.'

Robert Hughes, *The Shock of the New: Art and the Century of Change*, Thames & Hudson, 1991

39

**The National Gallery, London
William Wilkins, 1832–38**

By very definition all public galleries
and museums with permanent
collections are store rooms of
artefacts that are judged to be of
historical and cultural significance.
This is especially so of the great
national galleries and never more
so than when they contain
masterpieces within the canon
of works making up the grand
tradition. It is here that the history
of art can be seen in the original
and during the 20th century these
powerful institutions have
accommodated major works of
modern and postmodern fine art
and design. Their influence is
incalculable.

Language and art and design history

There is no single history of the visual arts, whatever might be suggested by the words used in titles such as, 'A History of Art', 'The History of Art' or 'A Brief History of Art'. This is born out by even the most cursory of glances at their contents lists, which reveal substantial inequalities: the prioritisation of one or some cultures over others; certain categories of art and design excluded altogether or the omission or marginalising of particular social or ethnic groups. Only professional artists and designers are included in the great majority of standard Western accounts. Even within these limits there is likely to be a further selectiveness: photography or academic painting unacknowledged in a book on 20th century fine art; handcrafted, or industrially produced objects alone but not appearing together in a book on design; or architect-designed but not commercial estate houses in a book on contemporary architecture. The language used in titles and subtitles can be misleading.

Language across
the disciplines

Language and art
and design history

Language and art
and design theory

Language
and ideology

Activity two

Summary

'isms

Semantic problems arising from the language used in book titles, subtitles and chapter headings, however, are minor compared with those confronting anyone engaging with the historical literature on 20th-century visual culture. Quite apart from the fact that the 20th century has seen new communication systems telescope world cultures into what is commonly called a global village, the number of art and design 'isms generated during this century has exceeded any before. From Fauvisme, Cubism and Futurism before the First World War, through Purism, Constructivism and Surrealism between the two World Wars, to Abstract Expressionism, Conceptualism and Minimalism later in the century, the list is so long that there are now books summarising the 'isms. Writers or commentators addressing the entire century, however selective they may be, also have to negotiate portmanteau terms such as 'Modernism' and 'Postmodernism'. The former is sufficiently distant in time to have acquired a substantial literature. The latter is still in dispute, as the alternative, hyphenated, 'post-modernism' suggests. Both of these 'isms have generated new vocabulary and concepts over the decades and they now shape the many standard accounts available.

Modernism

By the end of the first chapter alone, Nikolaus Pevsner in his *Pioneers of the Modern Movement* (original title 1936, revised and republished as *Pioneers of Modern Design*, 1960) has introduced at least ten key words or concepts by which he sought to define the new characteristics of modern art and design. More than half a century later, but by the same point in his book, *Modernism* (Phidaon Press, 2001), Richard Weston has nearly doubled the number of new terms used. Both authors, like so many others who have written about the modern period, adopted the increasingly specialised language that has come to signify Modernism, like *functionalism* (fulfilling the required needs), mass-production (production for the majority rather than the minority), standardisation (the regularisation of components in an assembly-line production system) and construction (the declaration of the supporting system over outward appearances), plus 'the untranslatable word *sachlich*, meaning at the same time pertinent, matter-of-fact, and objective, (which) became the catchword of the growing Modern Movement', as Pevsner correctly observed. Almost all of these and many other terms were acquired from other specialist disciplines, often other languages, and most are metaphorical. They function as images of what they seek to identify. This is very much the case with Le Corbusier's demand that the house be 'a machine for living in'.

40

The Bauhaus, Dessau, workshop wing and driveway Walter Gropius, 1925–26

This is one of the earliest examples of mature Modernist architecture. It is also the school of design where Modernist ideas were central to the curriculum. Designs by the students were sold as prototypes during the later 1920s, adding to the dissemination of Modernist ideals.

There can be little doubt that this accumulation of novel terminology was a necessary response to the emphasis placed upon innovation by leading artists and designers both in their creative visual work and in the proliferation of manifestos and theoretical texts written by them or their supporters. In retrospect, it might appear odd that in their desire to rid themselves of all traditional cultural assumptions about art and design, – especially the expectation that a picture should illustrate a story – the Modernists should have rejected the intrusions of literature into their own area of expertise while taking up writing themselves. But, as we all know, the unfamiliar is often very challenging and demands explanation. The innovations of modern art and design required commentary, even justification. The links between language and the visual arts could be re-established, albeit on new terms, and a new name given to these innovators; the *avant-garde* (those in the forefront of influence).

41

The Frankfurt kitchen
Grethe Schutte-Lihotzky, 1926

From the late 19th century onwards, women were major contributors to the ergonomics of domestic design. Arranging the relationship between storage, preparation, cooking and cleaning in the kitchen in an efficient way was given special attention. It was part of the Modernist preoccupation with functionalism.

Language across
the disciplines

Language and art
and design history

Language and art
and design theory

Language
and ideology

Activity two

Summary

**Isometric drawing of Walter
Gropius's design for the office
of the Bauhaus director
Herbert Bayer, 1923**

Orthogonal structures (elements
set at 90-degree angles) in two and
three dimensions are a marked
characteristic of Modernist art and
design. Isometric projection reveals
this in a way that linear perspective
would not, for elements that are
parallel in reality remain so in
their drawn presentation. The
asymmetric arrangement of the
furniture and fittings within this
three-dimensional grid is parallel
to the asymmetric arrangement
of components in a Modernist
painting.

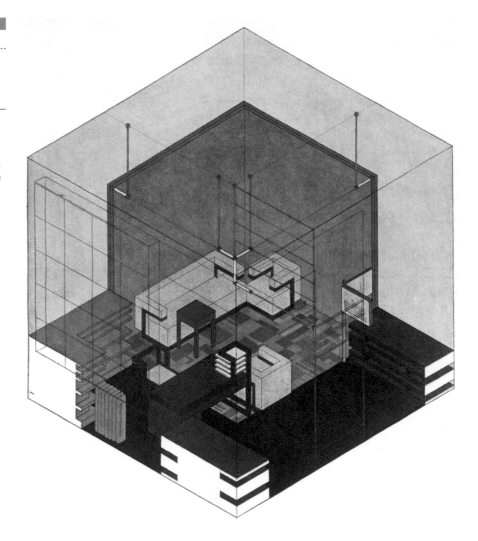

43

**Bottle of Vieux Marc, Glass, Guitar
and Newspaper
Pablo Picasso, 1913**

The flat, overlapping planes that
give depth while acknowledging
the fundamental flatness of the
picture surface exemplify a central
feature of Modernist writing on
fine art especially that of Clement
Greenberg (see facing page) and his
followers. They emphasised those
characteristics that distinguished
painting from the other arts.

Inflecting the modern

The several inflections of the word 'modern' are highly significant in themselves. In ordinary usage the semantic distinctions between these are blurred, but within art and design history, theory and criticism they have increasingly conveyed much more specific meanings. The primary meaning of modern denotes the present or recent times. In this sense, all artefacts produced during the same period, whether traditional or innovative in character, can be said to be modern. 'Modernity' is more narrowly defined and is used to identify the condition of being modern, especially in its more conscious progressive aspects.

'Modernism', like most other 'isms, identifies a set of ideas and practices. These are highly selective, opposed not only to traditional approaches but to those other contemporary, innovative developments that do not conform to its own ideals. These are: rationalism (the prioritisation of reason over all other means of explanation), regularisation (the most rational forms: square, rectangle, triangle, circle and the 90-degree angled grid, the orthogonal, whether two- or three-dimensional), and the technological (those elements of art, architecture or design derived from the applied sciences). These were the ideals promoted by Pevsner and others and recorded and commented upon by Weston.

'Modernist' denotes a person or artefact that supports these ideals. In Anglophone cultures, *moderne* (the French word for modern) is sometimes used to designate the popularisation of the decorative within modernity (rejected by Modernism) that is most readily associated with Art Deco, a term derived from the 1925 Paris Exposition Internationale des Arts Décoratifs et Industriels Modernes.

Reductive practices

Despite a revised text that included material on Art Nouveau, Futurism and Expressionism, all excluded in the original publication, Pevsner's foreword (in his *Pioneers of Modern Design*, 1960) still insists that his heroes, such as Adolf Loos and Walter Gropius, 'were the initiators of the style of the century and that Gaudí and Sant'Elia were freaks and their inventions fantastical rantings'. This is explicit critical-evaluation not objective history, but it makes abundantly clear that Art Nouveau and Futurism along with Expressionism, all decidedly innovative in their differing ways, were anathema to the Modernist cause and would later be labelled irrationalist.

A parallel and equally critical selection ultimately determined what came to be accepted as Modernist fine art. If painting and sculpture were to extricate themselves from the other arts and achieve some degree of autonomy they must, of necessity, concentrate upon what was most peculiar to their specialist area of practice. In Western painting, this constituted the formal elements and their effects and the flat surface on which these formal elements appeared. Very early in the 20th century Roger Fry and Clive Bell, following in the Formalist footsteps of Wölfflin, had concentrated attention on what Bell called 'significant form', distinguishing it from what were seen to be other, extraneous aspects of interest. This reductive approach reached its ultimate definition in Clement Greenberg's essay, 'Modernist Painting' (1960): 'flatness, two-dimensionality, was the only condition painting shared with no other art, and so Modernist painting oriented itself to flatness as it did to nothing else.'

Traditional ties

The standard accounts of Modernism through most of the 20th century are almost invariably partisan and even prescriptive. The language employed inclines to the rhetorical, capitalising on the connotative effects of metaphor and simile rather than logical argument to persuade the reader to accept a particular point of view. Ironically, for all its prioritising of new ideas and practices, Modernism perpetuated some long-established traditions, including a hierarchical critical evaluation that determined which artists, architects and designers should be considered a 'master', which artefacts qualified as a 'masterpiece', and which of these to include in an exemplary 'canon', albeit of Modernist works. A quick scan of the illustrations in these accounts is sufficient to alert us to who and what is being given preferential treatment.

Postmodernism

Postmodernism, or Post-modernism, hyphenated or not, may very well pose more problems of interpretation than Modernism. Like the term Post-impressionism, it can signify a historical period, a reaction to the previous 'ism, or a distinct cultural identity. However, unlike the earlier terms Impressionism, Post-impressionism and Modernism, we are, perhaps, too closely engaged in recent cultural changes to collectively decide upon the parameters of these particular ones.

A general history of Postmodernism embracing most of the visual arts, however selectively, has yet to be written. There are books that address Postmodern developments in fine art, architecture or design but these have circumspect titles such as, *After Modern Art*, *Architecture After Modernism*, or more directly, *The Art of Today*. Michael Collins's *Towards Post-Modernism: Design Since 1851* (British Museum Press, second revised edition, 1987) and *Post-Modern Design* (Rizzoli International Publications, 1990) are rare exceptions.

44

Vitra Design Museum poster
Mendell & Oberer, 1999

Design histories are diverse in content, sometimes focused on one production method such as industrial design, or one category of objects, such as chairs. At Vitra, a whole museum is devoted to chairs irrespective of their materials, methods of production or design. The poster, using the ubiquitous Modernist grid, directly reflects this.

Vitra Design Museum Collection

02 Formal language: the academic disciplines of art and design   Academic language

**Groninger museum, Netherlands
Coop Himmelblau, 1990–94**

Rejecting the rectilinearity and
undecorated surfaces of Modernist
architecture, this building appears
so unstable that it could be splitting
open, even falling apart. Intersecting
diagonal planes create a precarious
effect while strident colour and
all-over pattern further remove the
building from traditional or
Modernist expectations.

**The thematic house,
the winter room
Charles Jencks, 1985**

'Architecture is a hybrid concern, a
mongrel or macaronic affair…its
essential heterogeneity has been
recognised since Vitruvius defined it
in the first century BC as
"Commodity, Firmness and Delight".
But these three, he continued, "must
be supplemented by a fourth which
is just as essential: the symbolic"'.

Charles Jencks, *Towards a Symbolic
Architecture: The Thematic House*,
Rizzoli, 1985

Destabilising modernism

In Collins's account, as in those of many
others, 'Pop Art', with its blurring of the
boundaries between high and low culture and
its embrace of consumerism, plays a pivotal
role. These terms, together with others such as
kitsch, camp, and funk, indicate a decisive
move away from what by the 1960s had
become the severely reductive characteristics
and language of the International Style
(Modernism in its most programmatic,
aestheticised form). This radical shift in
sensibility is summed up in Robert Venturi's
riposte, 'Less is a bore', to Mies van der Rohe's,
'Less is more'. This shift is also reflected in the
choice of name by the founders of the 1981
Milan-based design group, Memphis, alluding
to a Bob Dylan song as well as both the
pop-music capital in Tennessee, USA, and the
ancient Egyptian urban civilisation.
Double-coding (or even treble or quadruple), as
Charles Jencks identified it, is the
superimposition of one meaning upon
another, thereby complicating the
interpretation of an artefact.

The burgeoning influence and example of
Saussurian linguistics during the same period,
as we have seen, contributed to this
destabilisation of received expectations in
visual culture. If language itself was insecurely
bonded to that which it sought to represent,
how could any authority be invested in any
statement? To what extent should historians
of visual culture trust the stated intentions of
artists, architects, designers or, for that matter,
theorists? Yet, Collins's very pertinent
observation that, 'the much-heralded "death
of the author" is not a commercial reality',
cannot be ignored in a consumer culture that
gives so much emphasis to the designer-label.

Language across
the disciplines

Language and art
and design history

Language and art
and design theory

Language
and ideology

Activity two

Summary

Alternatives

Once doubts arise about the authority of language to communicate a certain meaning, all verbal statements are open to a plurality of interpretation. Uncertainty leads to scepticism. This scepticism is as visible in the artefacts of Postmodernism as it is legible in the historical commentaries. Mike Featherstone in his 1991 book *Consumer Culture and Postmodernism* characterised several postmodern characteristics as: 'The effacement of the boundary between art and life; the collapse of hierarchical distinctions between high and mass/popular culture; a stylistic promiscuity favouring eclecticism and the mixing of codes; parody, pastiche, irony, playfulness and the celebration of the surface "depthlessness" of culture; the decline of the originality/genius or artistic producer; and the assumption that art can only be repetition.' Robert Venturi had promoted the *appropriation* of elements from the past, especially the more symbolic ones, in opposition to the purged world of Modernism and clearly linked this to the wider readmittance of historicism (the appearance, form or structure of historical styles). These characteristics are closely linked to pastiche and parody.

The two might best be distinguished in the context of cross-dressing. The drag artist relies upon our awareness that it is a 'fella in a frock' (or woman in trousers). It is an exaggeration of the stereotypical female or male characteristics: it is parody. The transvestite usually aims to be a convincing equivalent of the opposite sex: this is pastiche.

Despite its use of classical columns and their recessed equivalents, pilasters, Venturi's National Gallery extension makes clear that it is not a classical building like the main gallery with its centralised portico echoing Palladio's Villa Rotonda. The columns nearest to the old building are packed together but as the eye moves further away, the columns get further apart until they cease altogether. The section of the extension most distant from the old building is so stripped down that it could qualify as Modernist. Add to this the exposed iron roofing over the main staircase which in effect quotes 19th-century engineering structures and the building as a whole can easily be seen to be hybrid (of mixed origin, heterogeneous), another common characteristic of Postmodernism.

47a

Sainsbury's wing extension, the National Gallery, London Robert Venturi architectural office, 1986–1991

47b

The riverside development, Richmond, Surrey, UK Quinlan Terry, 1984–87

The parallels of pastiche and parody in visual culture are not difficult to spot: Quinlan Terry's Riverside development at Richmond-upon-Thames in the UK is pastiche – it looks like the traditional vocabulary of classical architecture. Robert Venturi's Sainsbury's Wing extension to the National Gallery, London, is parody.

48
- -
Colour collage
J M Clarke, 2007

Perhaps the most widely read theoretical books and essays on visual culture are those addressing the subject of colour. Traditionally considered in the West as the most emotive element and set in opposition to the more measurable line and form, there is no obvious consensus of theoretical opinion beyond a few basics. These are most often demonstrated on the ubiquitous colour circle and carry their own vocabulary, such as tonal, harmonious, contrasting or complementary colours. All are evident in this collage.

Language and art and design theory

According to the *Shorter Oxford Dictionary*, theory is primarily concerned with speculation, a mental scheme of things to be done, a systematic statement of rules or principles, or the formulation of abstract or speculative thought. Examples of all these definitions can be found within the theories of visual culture during the last hundred years. The language employed, however, does not always match either the objectivity or precision that this definition suggests. It can, sometimes, be as calculated as that of a scientific thesis. It can be almost entirely prescriptive, a set of rules for achieving a desired end. Or, it can be as rhetorical as any fictional text, more concerned to persuade the reader to a particular point of view than rationally argue the case for that position.

Language across
the disciplines

Language and art
and design history

Language and art
and design theory

Language
and ideology

Activity two

Summary

The future

'We will sing of great crowds excited by work, by pleasure, and by riot; we will sing of the multicoloured, polyphonic tides of revolution in modern capitals; we will sing of the vibrant mighty fervour of arsenals and shipyards blazing with violent electric moons; greedy railway stations that devour smoke-plumed serpents; factories hung on clouds by the crooked lines of their smoke; bridges that stride the rivers like giant gymnasts, flashing in the sun with the glitter of knives; adventurous steamers that sniff the horizon; deep-chested locomotives whose wheels paw the tracks like the hooves of enormous steel horses bridled by tubing; and the sleek flight of planes whose propellers chatter in the wind like banners and seem to cheer like an enthusiastic crowd.'

Of the 11 listed aims in Filippo Tommaso Marinetti's (1876–1944) *Founding Manifesto of Futurism* (1909), this is both the longest and most sustained example of rhetorical rather than rationalised exposition of a theoretical position. The initial 'We' was a fiction (there were no other members of the Futurist group at the time); verbal images, whether similes or metaphors, accumulate but without any suggestion of how these might be visually realised (what method should be used to represent 'greedy railway stations that devour smoke-plumed serpents'?); progressive technology is celebrated but through metaphorical, anthropomorphic and zoomorphic parallels ('bridges that stride the rivers like giant gymnasts' and 'the hooves of enormous steel horses bridled by tubing'). Paradoxes abound but the intended, incantatory effect is achieved.

Having already announced that, 'a roaring car…is more beautiful than the Victory of Samothrace' (the famous sculpture of a winged female figure with fluttering drapery), and that, 'We will glorify war – the world's hygiene,' as well as 'destroy the museums, libraries, academies of every kind', Marinetti concludes, 'Art, in fact, can be nothing but violence, cruelty, and injustice.' All of this is bombast, exaggerated statements whose primary aim is to arouse and excite instead of convince with rational argument.

The spiritual

Wassily Kandinsky's (1866–1944) *Concerning the Spiritual in Art* (1912), despite its consistent references to supposedly rational supporting evidence (Marxism, Theosophy, atonal music), depends for its effect upon an equally rhetorical use of highly metaphoric language: 'Colour is the keyboard, the eyes are the hammers, the soul is the piano with many strings. The artist is the hand that plays, touching one key or another purposively, to cause vibrations in the soul.' Kandinsky's claim in the next paragraph that: 'It is evident therefore that colour harmony must rest ultimately on purposive playing upon the human soul; this is one of the guiding principles of internal necessity' is pure speculation, its unsupported assertions underlined later in statements such as, 'form is the external expression of inner meaning'.

Many of Kandinsky's claims relate to his preoccupation with *synaesthesia*, the overlapping of one sensory response with another. Language itself betrays our common acceptance that a particular colour can be hot or cold, sweet or sour, soft or hard, quiet or loud. Kandinsky was himself acutely sensitive to these sensory associations and relies upon our (albeit Western) collective experience when he writes, 'yellow is the typically earthly colour', 'blue is the typically heavenly colour', before considering 'the varied powers of red'.

But where Marinetti's aspirations were for an urban-industrial renewal of visual culture, Kandinsky's, perhaps even more ambitiously, were for an apocalyptic, spiritual transformation of lived experience: 'Painting is a thundering collision of different worlds, intended to create a new world in, and from, the struggle with one another, a new world which is the work of art' (Wassily Kandinsky, *Reminiscences*, 1913). The language is biblical, more the Book of Revelations than a manual on painting.

02 Formal language: the academic disciplines of art and design   Academic language

A Futurist evening in Milan
Umberto Boccioni, 1911

Futurist evenings were emblematic of the movement as a whole: deliberately provocative, aggressive and iconoclastic, several different activities taking place simultaneously. Preoccupied with the dynamics of urban-industrial developments and the social and cultural changes entailed, the Futurists aimed to celebrate perpetual motion whether in essentially static paintings and sculptures or more temporal music and performance.

50

Impression No. 3 (Concert)
Wassily Kandinsky, 1911

A close friend of the innovative composer Arnold Schoenberg, Kandinsky was deeply interested in the parallels between music and painting, eventually creating an abstract art that is as independent of the usual appearances of the world as music is of the sounds of the world. Kandinsky was interested in synaesthesia, he believed colours could invoke sounds and that it was possible to 'hear' the colours in a painting. Impression No. 3 invites us to try.

Language across
the disciplines

Language and art
and design history

Language and art
and design theory

Language
and ideology

Activity two

Summary

The modern

Kandinsky is rightly regarded as a pioneer of abstraction in the visual fine arts, but before the First World War he cautioned against moving too quickly in this direction, fearful that non-figurative shapes and forms might be confused with the decorative arts. Ironically, 19th-century design theorising was much preoccupied with what constituted good surface design.

Owen Jones's *Grammar of Ornament* (1856) is central to this concern. Of his 37 'propositions', number eight, prophetically Modernist, states, 'all ornament should be based upon a geometrical construction'. Number 13 states that: 'flowers or other natural objects should not be used as ornaments, but conventional representations founded upon them sufficiently suggestive to convey the intended image to the mind, without destroying the unity of the object they are employed to decorate.' In other words, selective abstraction and flatness are the ideal much as Modernist fine art theory would promote.

This sympathetic, if reformist, theorising of decoration was to be eclipsed by the Viennese architect, designer and writer, Adolf Loos (1870–1933). His *Ornament is Crime* (1908) uncompromisingly states that, 'cultural evolution is synonymous with the removal of ornament from articles in daily use.' Coupled with the American architect Louis Sullivan's (1856–1924) earlier assertion that, 'form ever follows function', they are, perhaps, the two most paradigmatic statements of early Modernism.

Modernist graphics

Jan Tschichold (1902–1974) is the quintessential Modernist graphic designer. The impact of his visit to the first Bauhaus exhibition in 1923 was decisive. The theories stated in his definitive *The New Typography* (1928) were already clearly outlined in the ten *elementare typographie* published in a special edition of the journal *Typographische Mitteilungen* (1925). The first three elements are decisive to his overall theory. They state that:

1 Typography is shaped by functional requirements.

2 The aim of typographic layout is communication (for which it is the graphic medium). Communication must appear in the shortest, simplest, most penetrating form.

3 For typography to serve social ends, its ingredients need internal organisation – (ordered content) as well as external organisation – (the typographic material properly related).

In the later, expanded and elaborated text, sans-serif types, standardised paper sizes, asymmetric orthogonal layouts, and the rejection of anything extraneous, least of all decorative, to the purpose of the design, were forcefully and prescriptively proposed. Tschichold later revised his position, but *Die Neue Typographie* (*The New Typography*) had already exercised its influence on both contemporaries and on Modernist theory as a whole.

Rüstem Pasa Mosque, Istanbul, Iznik ceramic mural (detail), 1561

Owen Jones's *Grammar of Ornament* (1856) is a worldwide survey and analysis of surface design from which he sought to establish general principles. This included Turkish Ottoman ornament, such as the stylised, flattened plants in this tiled mural.

52

Moller house, ladies' lounge Adolf Loos, 1928

Although Loos banished any applied ornament or decoration, he incorporated the natural grain and pattern of various woods and marbles as well as painting selected walls in strong colours, as in this house.

53

'Kiki' poster, Jan Tschichold, 1927

Tschichold's early theories of graphic design and the examples he used to illustrate his book are a cornerstone of Modernist design in general. Undecorated, geometric, reduced to essentials and arranged asymmetrically in a grid composition, they aimed to fulfil the Modernist ideals of functionalist requirements.

NORMA TALMADGE

IN

KiKi

PHOEBUS PALACE

SHOWING AT . . . 400 615 830
SUNDAYS . . . 145 400 615 830

54

Bauhaus press letterhead Lázló Moholy-Nagy, c.1920

Fine artist, photographer and film-maker, designer, writer and influential teacher at the Bauhaus, Moholy-Nagy's graphic design was a very close parallel to that of Tschichold, especially in its reductiveness, and its asymmetrical but orthogonal alignment: the grid.

Language across
the disciplines

Language and art
and design history

Language and art
and design theory

Language
and ideology

Activity two

Summary

Roman Las Vegas

Learning From Las Vegas: The Forgotten Symbolism of Architectural Form (MIT Press, 1977), written with Denise Scott Brown and Steven Izenour, was Robert Venturi's second challenge to Modernism. At the outset, it makes its central concern clear, 'Las Vegas is analysed…only as a phenomenon of architectural communication.' Overall, the message is equally clear: just as academic architects went to study in Rome, contemporary students should go to Las Vegas, and the similarities and dissimilarities are explored in some detail.

Like the earlier work, much of the writing is structured around the use of comparisons and contrasts. This is especially so when the preferred, 'flamboyant' commercial buildings of the hedonistic gambling town are set in opposition to the 'puristic' austerities of the Modernist International Style. But another significant and consistent comparison, no doubt greatly influenced by the rise of Pop art, is with the Roman: 'The Italian landscape has always harmonised the vulgar and the Vitruvian,' that is to say, mixed high and low cultural elements. This is an important characteristic of Postmodernism, widely practised and frequently addressed in the relevant literature.

As with other important writers on Postmodern architecture, such as Charles Jencks's *The Language of Postmodern Architecture* (*Academy Editions*, 1977) Venturi and his colleagues argue that the symbolic level of interpretation is as essential in architecture as a formal or technical one. Adopting the concepts and tools of semiology, Venturi argues that, 'Architecture depends in its perception and creation on past experience and emotional association and that these symbolic and representational elements may often be contradictory to the form, structure, and program with which they combine in the same building.'

Overall, the language employed is as rich and varied as the thesis: academic mixed with the conversational, technical with the colloquial. Metaphors and similes abound. Signs 'inflect'. There are 'dumb' doorknobs and several neologisms, such as 'sprawl city'. In a book with so many comparisons and contrasts, binary opposites proliferate, a number going beyond the single word to opposing phrases, as in 'ugly and ordinary' against 'heroic and original', 'symbols in space' against 'forms in space' or 'mixed media' against 'pure architecture'.

Very early in Venturi's *Learning from Las Vegas: The Forgotten Symbolism of Architectural Form*, the major highway of the town is established as one of the main components in the overall argument:

'Las Vegas is to The Strip what Rome is to the Piazza…the zone of the highway is a shared order. The zone off the highway is an individual order. The elements of the highway are civic. The buildings and signs are private. In combination they embrace continuity and discontinuity, going and stopping, clarity and ambiguity, cooperation and competition, the community and rugged individualism….The agglomeration of Caesar's Palace and The Strip as a whole approaches the spirit if not the style of the late Roman Forum with its eclectic accumulations.… For three days one may imagine oneself a centurion at Caesar's Palace.'

Robert Venturi, *Learning from Las Vegas: The Forgotten Symbolism of Architectural Form*, MIT Press, 1977

56
- -
Bookshelf

As a form of enquiry, ideology is
concerned with the origin or nature
of ideas. An ideology is a system of
ideas and an ideologue is a theorist
of these. It follows, therefore, that a
substantial number of academic
disciplines, especially philosophy,
psychology, linguistics,
anthropology and sociology, are
relevant to and even overlap with
the history, theory and criticism of
visual culture. Many influential
writers from these overlapping
areas of study can be identified
among the collection of books in
this photograph. They are also
among the most frequently cited
authors in contemporary discourse.

Language and ideology

Among the most frequently used, contemporary ideological bases in the history, theory and criticism of visual culture are those associated with the diagnoses of Karl Marx (1818–83), Sigmund Freud (1856–1939) and Ferdinand Saussure (1857–1913). Whether from a sociological, psychoanalytical or linguistic point of view, these three have exercised sustained influence. However ideologically distinguished by their concepts and vocabulary, elements from all three are often eclectically combined in commentaries on contemporary visual culture.

Language across
the disciplines

Language and art
and design history

Language and art
and design theory

Language
and ideology

Activity two

Summary

What does possession mean to you?

7% of our population own 84% of our wealth

The Economist, 15 January, 1966

57

Possession?
Victor Burgin, 1976

Adopting the commercial poster format with its photograph and text for fine art purposes, this highly conceptualised image is a good example of how influences from semiology can be successfully combined with social concern. The ambiguities of the photographic image are exposed through the simple device of a question and answer textual accompaniment that subverts any positive reading of the visual evidence.

The sociological

Within contemporary discourse on visual culture, a sociological approach is no longer restricted to the concepts and vocabulary of Karl Marx as were, to a great extent, the monumental volumes of Arnold Hauser's *Social History of Art* (Routledge, 1965). The issue of class struggle has been overtaken by something even more ideological.

For Marxists, the artefacts of art and design are products, and artists and designers are part of a wider division of labour. The utilitarian, or *use value*, of a painting or sculpture may differ from that of a spade or spoon, but not fundamentally. Utilitarian objects, commodities, just as readily acquire the status and prestige of *symbolic value* as objects of fine art; the social and cultural distinctions attributed to them function in the same way. Symbolic values support hierarchies. For Marxists, power and authority are held by those who own the material resources; the means of production and of distribution. Workers sell their labour. The (metaphorical) material base, the entire economic structure, determines the *superstructure*, the socio-cultural institutions and their practices. The ideology of the ruling class is a justification for this social system.

As we have seen, the dominant ideology (by appearing to be natural, given, and not a cultural construct), mythologises the values of those in power. Antonio Gramsci further explored the power of ideology, the extent to which cultural practices internalised by a majority exercise as much collective, controlling influence, a hegemony, as legal or physical force. Revealing these collusive practices is often the motivation of Marxist artists and designers. Exposing these same practices is what some historians and critics of visual culture do.

The psychoanalytical

Like Marxism, psychoanalytical theory since Sigmund Freud has passed through many revisions and several alternatives, each addition and transformation adding to the already existing concepts and vocabulary. Essential to all of these is the common belief, now absorbed into common usage, that there exists a conscious and sub-conscious level in the human psyche. What often interests those engaged in visual culture is the degree to which the conscious intentions of an artist or designer are determined by their sub-conscious aspirations and anxieties. Psychoanalytical commentaries seek to discover these hidden intentions, often using methods similar to those of the psychoanalyst's *free association* technique, a method entirely dependent upon the analyst's response to the highly ambiguous, given material.

Initially, Freud divided the psyche, uppermost down, into conscious, pre-conscious and unconscious levels with a system of censorship operating between each level. By the early 1920s, he had reconfigured this relationship and presented a new structure and vocabulary: in reverse order these are the *id* as the source of all undifferentiated desire or fear; the *superego* as the internalised force of cultural repression; the *ego* as the determining relationship between both of these factors. Central to this repressive, psychic mechanism is the concept of psychological castration, the *Oedipal Complex*, in which the infant male's desire to possess its all-providing mother is threatened by both mother and father.

Post-Freudian analysts such as Melanie Klein and Jacques Lacan have reinterpreted several of Freud's concepts. Klein focused attention upon the pre-verbal stages of the child's development, especially behavioural responses to the breast. Together with Joan Riviere they diagnosed the patterns of love, hate and reparation that have influenced many writers on art, including Adrian Stokes and Richard Wollheim.

The more recent theories of Jacques Lacan, true to his post-Saussurian origins, recognised that, given the fundamentally verbal relationship between analyst and analysand in the traditional circumstances of psychoanalysis, the human psyche was best understood through linguistic models. Decoding the dreams and incoherent statements of analysands was parallel to that of decoding any language statement and, by a semiological shift, the visual. Even the so-called 'mad' person was still using language, however unconventionally. On which basis, it is easy to see how this approach could be applied to the albeit different means of visual communication. Like Freud, Lacan divided the psyche into three 'orders'. All have had ready application to visual culture. They are: the imaginary: the *mirror stage*, that moment of self-recognition as separate from the mother; the symbolic: the moment the child enters language, culture, and encounters the significance of the father (*patriarchy*); the real: the illusive, never-defined, unstable notion of being.

58

**PPDVI
(Post-Partum Document,
Documentation VI: pre-writing
alphabet, exurgue and diary)
Mary Kelly, 1978**

Each section in the Post-Partum Document series uses a different structure but Kelly's overall concern is always with the relationship between her and her son during the weaning period. The section VI series use the format of the Rosetta Stone as a structural model and focuses on Lacan's 'symbolic order', the moment of the child's entry into language and learning to write. It is also the final stage in the Oedipal Complex. A significant feature of the whole series is the absence of any images of the body, the mother's or the child's.

Feminist identity

In discussions of *identity*, the concept of *the other* plays a major role, for the notion of self depends upon an awareness of what is not self. In Western binary thought, female and feminine are the contraries of male and masculine, the latter pair prioritised over the former in a male-dominated patriarchal culture. Conventional definitions of gender identity have consistently assumed an essentialist or foundational position committed to the concept of the universally feminine, a condition given at birth. Although there are those who continue to maintain this or similar positions, this concept has been increasingly challenged, especially in the context of Postmodernism. Gender identity, as with all other identities, it is argued, is not a naturally given thing, the same in all places at all times, but a social and cultural construction. The Postmodern concepts of difference and the more extreme incommensurable (incompatible, irreconcilable) are decisive here.

Judith Butler is a central figure in current discourse on gender. For her, there is no fixed identity of any kind and no identity independent of our phallocentric, patriarchial (male-dominated) society. She asserts that 'identity is *performatively* constituted by the very expressions that are said to be its results'. Most individuals behave in a way that fulfils what is expected of them. Gender constructions are fabrications, performative operations; at the lowest level, role-play.

These ideas have radically changed not only many interpretations of representations of women, but how women artists represent themselves and others. Freud had noted that the act of looking was decisive in the awareness of sexual difference (the female lack of a penis). As we have seen, for Lacan, the infant's first awareness of self-identity was also in the act of looking; seeing its reflection in a mirror or other surface. It is not surprising that within visual culture *scopophilia* (the delight in looking) should have taken on considerable importance. For Laura Mulvey (*Visual Pleasure and Narrative Cinema, Screen*, Vol.16, Iss.3, 1975) *the gaze* itself is always genderised. Traditionally, the vast amount of representations of women have been by (heterosexual) men for other (heterosexual) men, and specific interests are at play throughout. The look is active. In recent decades, a number of women artists have adopted different ways of subverting conventional expectations.

Gay identity

Parallel and sometimes overlapping developments can be identified within the Gay Liberation Movement and its connections with visual culture. To come out of the closet is to be publicly seen as a homosexual, a gay man or lesbian woman. Visual images are sometimes said to be gay or feminist but the possible existence of a gay or feminist aesthetic is a contested proposition. Neither group is unified in theory or practice; pluralism is characteristic of both and extends to formative influences and formal outcomes.

One significant development is that of Queer Theory, which embraces not only male and female homosexuality but bisexuality, transsexual and transgenderised, as well as other identities. Postmodernist culture has been divided into one of resistance or reaction. The latter relates to assimilation, the absorption of whatever difference into the status quo. The former rejects assimilation and all its normative demands. In appropriating the pejorative term 'queer' as a positive one for itself, Queer Theory made a feature of its resistance. Gay and other artists have found ways of incorporating this resistance into their representations.

Sometimes I come to hate people because they can't see... I've gone empty, completely empty and all they see is... my arms and legs, my face, my height and posture, the... from my throat. But I'm fucking empty. The person I... ago no longer exists; drifts spinning slowly into the... way back there. I'm a xerox of my former self. I can't... dying any longer. I am a stranger to others and to myself... to pretend that I am familiar or that I have history... I am glass, clear empty glass. I see the... through me. I see people... by constant population... mistaken for my... moving... no longer... an empty... I am... empty... stopped... touch me... another... I try to... my lips among the... I'm a dark smudge... glass human disappearing in... waving my invisible arms and legs. I am shouting my invisible words. I am getting so weary. I am growing tired. I am waving to you from here. I am crawling and looking for the aperture of complete and final emptiness. I am vibrating in isolation among you. I am screaming but it comes out like pieces of clear ice. I am signaling that the volume of all this is too high. I am waving. I am waving my hands. I am disappearing. I am disappearing but not fast enough.

59

Untitled no 122
Cindy Sherman, 1983

The most consistent feature of Sherman's work is the use of herself as model for her photographs. Her earliest work, just like this later one, used the film-still format, a significant moment that invited narrative readings. Each image, however, presents a different character, raising questions about just how fixed is identity as well as suggesting that it might be something acted out – what Butler called the performative.

60

Untitled
David Wojnarowicz,1992

A gay activist, Wojnarowicz is decidedly within the resistance category of Postmodernism. Like a number of other artists during the last three decades, he combines text and photographic image, manipulating these to address difficult issues in as direct a way as possible. Here, he confronts the prejudiced view at the time that AIDS was a gay disease (Wojnarowicz died from AIDS in 1992) by compounding the gestures of a beggar with those of a sick man i.e. a gay man. The text is from the artist's own book *Memories That Smell Like Gasoline* (Artspace Books, 1992).

Racial identity

The term 'Western culture' presupposes other cultures and otherness is a central issue in contemporary discourse on racial as on other kinds of identity. If all identity is culturally constructed, the identities of non-white people raise some very specific issues. Given the powerful role of written language within Western culture, those from oral cultures without written records, documents or literature were and sometimes still are judged inferior. The adoption of another's written language complicates matters further. This is paralleled in the context of visual culture too and verbalised through the familiar use of implicit, if not always explicit, binary terms. Until very recently, Western writing interpreted sub-Saharan African, wooden figures as primitive carvings by anonymous craftsmen; Brancusi's equally conceptualised, wooden pieces as sophisticated sculptures by a named artist. The disparity between the two evaluations was blatant. Disparities of this kind, and others, still persist.

Post-colonialism

European colonialism was not a worldwide phenomenon, but its *imperialist*, universalising ambitions are readily recognisable in those of contemporary globalisation; the willing or forceful establishment of Western, capitalist, Liberal-democratic values. In this context difference acquires other meanings, including the incommensurable (the incompatible, irreconcilable), for example, the clash of fundamentalist Islam and equally fundamentalist Christianity. Despite the common origins of the Christian, Islamic and Jewish faiths, questions of identity whether religious, social or sexual have become acute. The postmodern assumption that *meta-narratives* (those universalising systems of belief or theory) are dead is clearly contradicted. If visual culture is to be addressed globally, these highly significant differences must be accommodated. Manifestations of these complexities are replete within visual culture and can be both supportive of and interrogative of Postmodernism.

61

Paris Match cover
Issue 326, 25 June–2 July, 1955

Precipitously close in time to the earliest dismantling of European colonial rule, the image was one Roland Barthes decoded in 'Myth Today', the concluding essay in *Mythologies* (Vintage, 1993 edition). His analysis focused on the way a young black soldier saluting is, in the context of the conservative magazine *Paris Match* and growing demands from the colonised for independence, used to legitimate French imperialism.

**Folie no L5, intersection of
the north-south axis and the
canal de l'Ourc
Bernard Tschumi, c.1985**

The red-painted *folies* at the Parc
de la Villette were, like the three
superimposed structures, left for
others to complete, further
removing any single, authorial
control. 'La Villette is a term in
constant production, in continuous
change; its meaning is never fixed
but is always deferred, differed,
rendered irresolute by the
multiplicity of meanings it
inscribes.'

Bernard Tschumi, *Architecture and
Disjunction*, The MIT Press, 1996.

Deconstruction

The claim that there is a single, correct
meaning or interpretation of a text or visual
image usually relies upon both knowledge of
the author's intentions and trust in the text's
ability to convincingly communicate this
single meaning. But this confidence is eroded
and eventually erased with the realisation that
the unfixed character of words themselves, as
of visual images too, undermines any trust in
the existence of unified messages.

The multiplicity of possible meanings
available in the interpretation of a text or
visual image is a prime concern in any
deconstructive reading. *Deconstruction* focuses
attention on the internal inconsistencies that
are always present, the rhetorical devices and,
in particular, the hierarchical assumptions
implicit in binary opposites such as nature
and culture, order and chaos, where the
meaning of either one in a pair is dependent
on the other but one is always prioritised.
Meanings are never fixed, they are always
open to differences of interpretation. Jacques
Derrida, the central figure in deconstruction,
coined the term *differance*, a neologism which
in French fuses the verbs to differ and to defer.
Differing interpretations of a text or visual
image result in meaning being endlessly
deferred.

**Superimposition of lines,
points and surfaces,
Parc de la Villette, Paris
Bernard Tschumi, c.1985**

Tschumi's relation to
deconstruction is not only through
his contacts with Jacques Derrida.
Tschumi wrote in *Architecture and
Disjunction* (The MIT Press, 1996) of
the Parc de la Villette that, 'the
superimposition of three coherent
structures can never result in a
supercoherent megastructure, but in
something undecidable, something
that is the opposite of totality'. This
diagram illustrates the separate
structures employed.

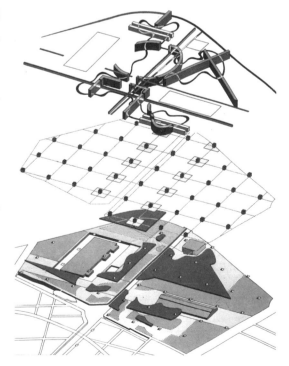

Language across
the disciplines   Language and art
and design history   Language and art
and design theory   Language
and ideology   Activity two   Summary

Activity two
How well does formal academic language communicate?

All interpretation of visual images presupposes a point of view. Assumptions about the historical and cultural context, the relationship with other images, what is significant and insignificant, are always made.

Examine each of these images and then make notes in answer to the following questions:

1 What, beyond their titles, would you say was the subject of the picture?

2 Which of the theoretical models described in this chapter (such as the sociological, the psychoanalytical, the feminist and so on) do you think might best help explain the image?

3 How differently do you think viewers from different social and cultural backgrounds might interpret the image?

4 What aspects of the image, if any, do you think relate to questions of class, race, or gender? How are these addressed?

5 How do you interpret the image?

64
Classical ruins
William Gowe Ferguson,
late 17th century

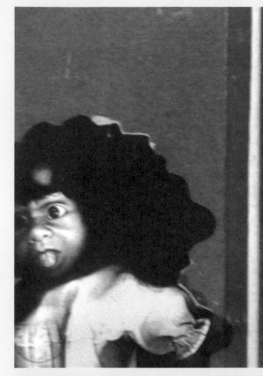
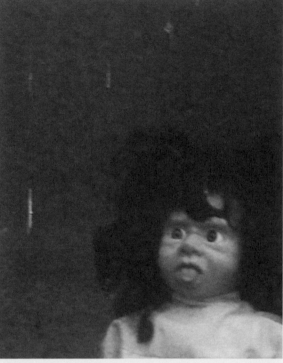

65
- -
Dolls, Dresden
Sebastian Loew, 2005

66
- -
Talking Presence
Sonia Boyce, 1988

Summary

1

All academic disciplines have their own specialist language.

2

The specialist language employed unavoidably determines understanding.

3

Dividing the history of art and design into periods, styles and movements is only an expedient.

4

There are no clear distinctions between the history, theory and criticism of visual culture.

7

The vocabulary particular to Modernism and Postmodernism is as much a part of their identities as the artefacts.

10

Theoretical writing can be prescriptive as well as explanatory.

5

The title of a book can be misleading about its content.

8

In the 20th century many more artists and designers took to writing their own theories. Is this an attempt to determine interpretation and understanding?

6

Histories of art and design are never neutral; they are always selective and written from a particular point of view.

9

The language of art and design theory is just as likely to use metaphorical and rhetorical devices as sequential logical statements.

Language across the disciplines

Language and art and design history

Language and art and design theory

Language and ideology

Activity two

Summary

03 Informal Language: beyond the academic disciplines

03

Informal language: beyond the academic disciplines

67

Why I chose graphic design (detail)
Jamie Howlett, 2005

In this illustrated conversation
between two figures at a bar, the
speech bubbles nicely contain not
only the kind of dialogue familiar to
art and design students but the kind
of language used too. It is almost
entirely colloquial from the casual
form of address, 'Hey', via the
elisions, 'what's' and 'that's', to the
whole tone, which is far removed
from the vocabulary of academic
speech or writing.

Colloquial language

In English, the distinction between formal or academic and informal or colloquial language has sometimes been explained by directing attention to the etymology (the origin of words) of the language used. Colloquial language is common speech and in ordinary conversations in English it is generally the case that most of the vocabulary has its origins in Anglo-Saxon or Germanic languages. In contrast, academic language relies heavily upon a vocabulary with origins in Latin or ancient Greek. It is the kind of language that readily identifies the learned professions and, because it can easily seem remote from everyday speech, makes classical literature sound impossibly elevated.

High and low language

The distinction between formal or academic and informal or colloquial language is not neutral. In Anglophone culture, those who speak and write with a vocabulary substantially derived from the Greco-Latinate tradition are easily distinguished from those whose speech and writing is almost exclusively from an Anglo-Saxon one. The former are recognised as a minority, well-educated, privileged and possibly an elite. The latter are the majority, largely educated in the common culture, the norm. Such distinctions, however, are not rigid: it is perfectly possible to belong to both groups. Just as many people can slip out of one language into another with ease, recognising the overlaps between them, many can embrace both high and low language cultures with equal ease. Some students quickly learn how to do all of these.

The following two quotations illustrate the distinction between colloquial and academic language:

'The core narratives that encode Western phallocentrism's political unconscious serve not merely to structure the study of the histories of art, but to establish a story of art as The Story of Art, the canonical legend of Western masculine Christian creativity which becomes synonymous with art, pure and simple.'

Griselda Pollock, *Vision and Difference: Feminism, Femininity and Histories of Art*, Routledge, 2003

and:

'It is bad design, not good design, that makes an impression. You notice toilets you can't step into because the door barely clears the seat, door handles you can't grip, buildings you get lost in. We ricochet from one design gaffe to another and yet we are told that "British design leads the world". Remind yourself of that fatuous slogan the next time you try to open an overloaded filing cabinet.'

Germaine Greer, *Guardian*, 13 March 2006

Both quotations are from texts written by academic, feminist, women writers, but for very different contexts. Griselda Pollock's book is addressed to academic readers, whether students or peer-group professionals. Words such as 'encoded', 'phallocentrism', 'canonical' and 'synonymous' are all of ancient Greek or Latin origin. Germaine Greer is here writing for the general reader of a national newspaper: it is journalism. Quite apart from the elision 'can't', widely used in ordinary conversation, words such as 'bad', 'door', 'handle' and 'loaded', are all of Anglo-Saxon or Germanic origin. But while this etymological distinction between formal and informal language is still of some value, it is complicated in contemporary academic discourse by the appropriation of words from diverse origins. *Flâneur* (French), used to identify the detached consumer of the urban spectacle, or *zeitgeist* (German), used to identify the spirit of the age, are good examples.

03 Informal Language: beyond the academic disciplines

Dyson vacuum cleaner

Asked by BBC television to comment on the Dyson vacuum cleaner, Germaine Greer wondered which one, 'upright, cylinder or ball? Yellow and purple, silver and yellow, lime green and purple – or none of the above?' Her judgement overall was that, 'As far as engineering is concerned, the Dyson is either loved or hated – but surely no one thinks any model is good looking…. Nothing was ever more plastic, gluey and ludicrously brittle.'

Greer's language avoids, as far as possible, the formal and academic. Every word in her BBC statement is familiar to the majority, even 'ludicrous' and 'plastic'. Although of Latin origin, 'ludicrous' has passed into ordinary Anglophone speech. In its original ancient Greek and its subsequent formal, academic meaning, 'plastic' identifies something malleable, as in clay or paint, but Greer uses it in its more recent meaning of something synthetic, unnatural, knowing perfectly well that all the Dyson vacuum cleaners are almost entirely composed from modern synthetic plastics. The rhetoric of her statement relies upon an association between the common language and common sense.

69

UK Takeover: volume 4
Album cover, 2006

The typography for the red title and the white repeat fringing the lower right figure are obviously adapted from the graffiti that is so closely associated with the music.

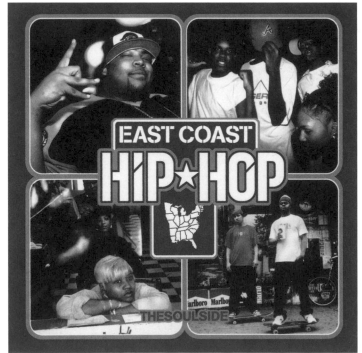

70

East Coast Hip Hop
Album cover, 2006

The photographic imagery is a catalogue of many elements identifying the subculture of Hip Hop and its links through graffiti with other groups such as skateboarders.

Language, culture and subculture

Academic disciplines are not alone in acquiring very specialised vocabulary and terminology. The subcultures within a single language culture do too and these can be as exclusive as any within academia. Colloquial language is no less exclusive than academic. In a different context, Greer's 'bad', as subcultural slang, can signify the opposite, much as the word 'wicked' has been used to mean good. No word ever has a fixed interpretation. Every verbal or visual statement is made within the context of other verbal and visual statements, as the theory of intertextuality makes very clear. The language patterns of any language culture inevitably contain common habits of speech familiar to the whole group. These patterns of speech are instantly recognisable: so much so that many members of the group can accurately anticipate the ending of another's sentence. As members of any one or more language cultures, we are also responsive to the many connotations of any single statement. A wider awareness of these possibilities gives rise to a more complex response and understanding.

All language cultures, therefore, presuppose high levels of response and understanding among a majority within the language group if communication is to be effective. This is just as true of any subcultural group as it is of a specialised academic one. The language within any of these groups is so particularised that it requires initiation. Serious problems of understanding can arise when the cultural or subcultural language used is not familiar. There is a parallel here in the visual arts. At any one time and in any one culture or subculture there are widely accepted types and categories of art and design that are acceptable and understood by a majority within a group. Any art and design that falls outside the received norms of any particular group is likely to be misunderstood. This is a problem that much contemporary art and design poses for a receiving audience and it is especially the case with our ubiquitous urban graffiti.

71

Punk identity

If language is a major bonding agent between members of the same language culture then the same is equally true of subcultural identities within the same dominant language culture. It is not only the differences in visual appearance that distinguish one subcultural group from another (few would confuse this image of a Punk with that of a Hippie), it is the language used by the group to discuss its identity that is different. Language is always specific to a particular socio-cultural context.

Language and difference

The direct translation of the vocabulary and concepts of one language into another is frequently impossible. Unsatisfactory approximations have to be found and these in turn influence understanding of what is being written or spoken about. Adrian Forty in his admirable and very pertinent book, *Words and Buildings: A Vocabulary of Modern Architecture* (Thames & Hudson, 2000), points out that for the single English word 'functional', German already had in the first decades of Modernism three: *sachlich*, generally translated as 'thingness'; *zwechmassig*, generally translated as 'purposeful'; and *funktionell*, the nearest to the English translation. In the predominantly German language culture of early Modernism, the connotations of each of these distinct words had significance. In English, they are lost.

Translated language

Compared with other languages, English is estimated to have by far the largest vocabulary, compiled as it is from diverse sources, especially the admixture of Anglo-Saxon and Greco-Latin words. This has advantages when Anglophones try to describe or explain an artefact for there are often nouns and adjectives in abundance. But this possibility has its limitations. Any language that has synonyms (words or phrases that stand as equivalents) for so many material and immaterial phenomena has the potential to be either more precise, by selecting the appropriate word for the required purpose, or an inconclusive rambling, by using words that do not approximate to what the speaker or writer seeks to describe or explain.

72

Skateboards

Customising the skateboard can be through consumer choice, independent design or both but the transitoriness of skateboard graphics, like graffiti, is evident here in the visible wear and tear.

73
....
Skateboarders
....

The connection between graffiti and skateboarding is evident in skateboard zines and the boards themselves. Here, graffiti is actually the site for skateboarding.

Beyond English

Each language culture is inevitably bonded to the wider culture. This is not the context in which to discuss the balance between the two. However, several key questions are of immediate importance: does the development of a culture generate the vocabulary and concepts required for that culture to define and discuss its major concerns, or does the ability of the language limit what can or cannot be said? Is a language culture reflective of the wider culture in all its dimensions? The relevant concern here is that all language cultures have their own advantages and disadvantages for both those within the culture and those dependent upon translation. In addition, each language culture has its own subcultures and each of these depends upon the acquisition of a very particularised vocabulary and concepts.

Unlike Western individualist, competitive culture, traditional Japanese culture is frequently described by Western commentators as deferential. The interests and concerns of the social group are prioritised over personal ones. This may be reflected in or determined by Japanese language structures. The Japanese seldom use the personal pronoun, 'I', and do not discriminate between the definite, 'the', and indefinite, 'a', article, nor do they always clearly distinguish between things in the singular, 'mouse', and plural, 'mice'. (English itself is not always clear here; compare 'fish', 'fowl' or 'deer'). Recognising these cultural differences is important and not only for the translator. Any statement addressed to a Japanese audience should be made with awareness of the cultural differences. This is also true of any other different language culture.

Icelandics have more than 20 words for different kinds of snow. Many non-Anglophone, European languages have separate verbs to distinguish between 'to know' and 'to know about', unlike English. German more readily allows the conversion of a concrete noun, *sachlich*, into an abstract one, *sachlichkeit*. Latinate languages, especially Italian, incline towards the generic (a class or category of objects or functions). In ordinary conversation, Italians will most likely refer to all mechanical equipment, be it washing machine, camera or motorcar, as *la machina*, the machine. Language is always peculiar to the cultural and subcultural context.

Alternative languages

All languages have their subcultures and each of these always depends upon the acquisition of a very particularised use of vocabulary and concepts. Colloquial language patterns in each specific subcultural group are vital to the construction of identity, just as are its visual and other manifestations. Within a subcultural group, the relationship between the verbal and visual is often an intimate one, each contributing to the creation of the specific identity.

During the second half of the 20th century, subcultural groups proliferated and especially so among the young. If, by definition, few of these original subcultures existed beyond a limited number of people and in a limited number of places, awareness of their existence and what they signified influenced many outside these limitations and continues to do so. Present-day, international students of visual culture are often more informed about these recent subcultures than they are about their own, native, historical cultures, whatever these may be, although the two are not necessarily exclusive.

The names of these subcultures have distinct denotatory and connotatory meanings. For example, the Beats (or Beatniks) appropriated the negative original meaning of the word 'beat' or 'beaten' and, therefore, associated with someone marginalised, for positive ends. If Jack Kerouac's 1957 novel *On the Road* epitomised the Beats' itinerant lifestyle and particular language, it is William Burroughs's cut-up literary technique (literally cutting up and collaging existing texts) that has had the greatest influence on both the verbal and visual patterns of subcultural graphic design. It has particularly influenced the writing and layout of fanzines (a literary product acting as an alternative to the established norm).

The Hippies are inseparable from the specifically subcultural concepts of the *alternative society* or *counter-culture* in which utopian ideals were used to confront the despised, capitalist consumerism of the 1960s. The same ideals are equally inseparable from a drug culture and the creation of psychedelic art and design (a hybrid mix of Art Nouveau biomorphic forms with a stridently acidic colour palette) together with a specific vocabulary, such as 'mind-blowing' and 'far out'.

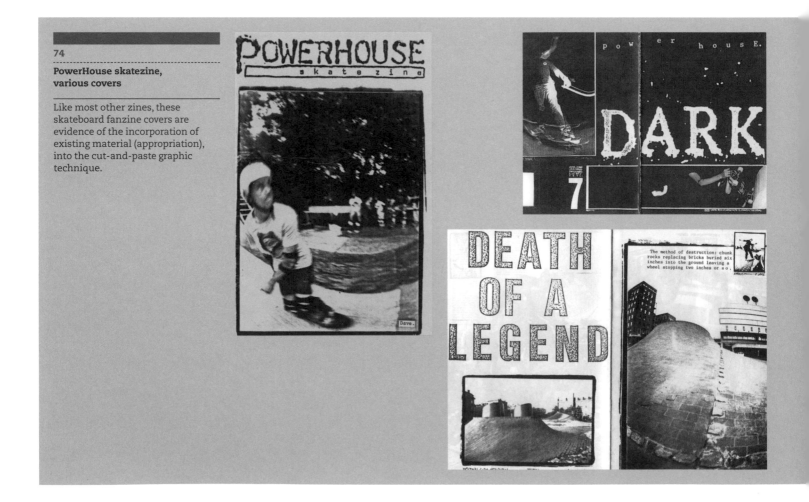

74

PowerHouse skatezine, various covers

Like most other zines, these skateboard fanzine covers are evidence of the incorporation of existing material (appropriation), into the cut-and-paste graphic technique.

In origin, the word 'Punk' signified something rotten or worthless but by the early 20th century it was associated with hooligans. This etymology was not lost on many who took the 1975 New York fanzine PUNK as their subcultural identity. Punks were openly provocative in every aspect of their appearance (bondage gear, spike-top or Mohican hair-do, the emblematic safety-pin), behaviour ('gobbing' or spitting at stage performers, 'pogoing', a vertical leaping dance with arms close to the body and derived from pogo-stick users), and graphic design. The characteristic, cut-and-paste collaging of *appropriated*, existing material was perfected in the work of Jamie Reid for the Sex Pistols band, but was typical of the many Punk fanzines.

At the time, these proliferating subcultures posed something more than an alternative; they were rightly perceived to be a potential threat to the established order. Although the possible challenge of these subcultural groups has subsequently been neutralised, both the verbal and visual vocabulary has influenced more recent subcultural groups, including Hip Hop, surfers, skateboarders and graffitists.

Zines

'Zines' (the abreviated word itself is significant) are both an identifiable category of publication and very particular to the sub-cultural group each represents. The particular vocabulary and concepts, like the characteristics of the overall layout, can vary considerably but the common factors are what Stephen Duncombe in his *Notes from Underground: Zines and the Politics of Alternative Culture* (Verso Books, 1997) defines as, 'the ethic of DIY, do-it-yourself: make your own culture and stop consuming that which is made for you.' They are, 'non-commercial, non-professional, small-circulation magazines that their creators produce, publish, and distribute by themselves.' They are, therefore, alternative, even counter to both established academic and popular publications just as their characteristic contents are the expression of marginalised groups.

Those who write and realise the zines are 'zinesters', not journalists or graphic designers, although they may be both, and contributors offering specific opinions on issues relevant to the readership write 'rants' rather than feature articles. Both the noun and the verb rant are of Dutch origin, closely linked to the Germanic rave, hence the original and contemporary association with frenzy. None of these meanings denotes or connotes the conventions of a rational, logically presented, point of view expected of most popular journalism.

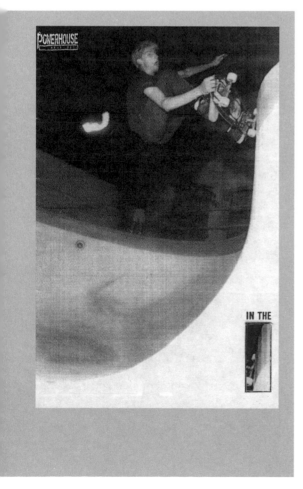

Hip Hop

Over the last two decades, Hip Hop has
become the most international, influential
subcultural group, having evolved from its
roots in 1970s New York black ghettos or
'hoods (neighbourhoods) into a richly
overlapping mix of words, music, dance, dress
and graphics. As with all other youth
subcultures, music is the core element
bonding its members. For Hip Hop this is Rap,
the rapid, rhythmically spoken monologue
over a musical background. The vocabulary
used in Rap is that of ordinary conversation
within the subculture. The music has clear
parallels with several aspects of postmodern
visual culture, especially the appropriation of
existing material for purposes different from
that of the original. Scratching is the dragging
of the needle across the tracks of commercial
recordings. Quickmixing is a collage of musical
fragments electronically lifted from different
sources. Sampling is a direct musical
equivalent to appropriation; a reworking of
readily recognisable examples.

Graffiti

The language of graffiti is extensive and every
bit as specialised as that of conventional fine
art. The word graffiti itself has ancient Greek
and Latin origins. *Graphein* in ancient Greek
compounds to draw, paint or write, as in to
describe or depict. The Latin, *graphium*, is the
tool used by scribes. *Graffiti* is Italian and
linked to *sgraffito*, a mural technique. There is
an obvious irony here.

Graffiti is as old as fine art, but where our
Western fine art tradition from the classical
through the Italian Renaissance to the present
is not only a legitimate but elevated cultural
form, graffiti is illegitimate, commonly
categorised with vandalism and likely to be
erased in as brief a time as it took to make.
A whole list of binary terms operate in any
discussion of graffiti: legal – illegal; amateur –
professional; high – low; honourable –
dishonourable; permanent – transitory. Just
when the complex, ghetto graffiti of New York
began to appear in the 1980s, one-time
graffitists such as Jean-Michel Basquiat and
Keith Haring were taken up by first
commercial and then public galleries,
legitimised and made artists.

Graffitists prefer to call themselves writers rather than artists, a term that makes them an identifiable member of the subculture, but one that consciously links them to words and even scribes. The key element in this is the writer's adopted name or signature, their *tag* (their real names necessarily concealed in an illegal activity). 'Tagging', along with 'hitting' or '*getting up*' are verbs for the writing activity. An 'up' is a prolific writer. After which, the subtleties of the vocabulary proliferate. Inevitably, those engaged in an illegal activity such as graffiti are disinclined to make public statements about what they do but there are revealing exceptions:

'If you had a piece in every borough, okay, as opposed to 50 or 60 tags in every borough, you would be considered more up really than the person with all the tags, although you haven't got as many pieces of art work.'
Drax, quoted in Nancy Macdonald, *The Graffiti Subculture: Youth, Masculinity and Identity in London and New York* (Palgrave Macmillan, 2001)

As with academic language, graffiti language requires initiation, but once initiated, Drax's statement above is easily decoded. A '*throwup*' is a rapid outline of a signature with just a black or white filling of the contours. A 'dub' has a silver or occasionally gold infilling. A 'piece' uses two or more colours. To 'drop' is to create a piece, to 'burn' is to do it exceptionally well, hence a '*burner*', the graffitists' equivalent of a masterpiece. 'Wildstyle' is the most complex writing style, easily identified by the tightly integrated, very nearly illegible letters.

Stencil graffiti
D:FACE, 2006

The term 'street art' has increasingly been used as a collective noun for a very diverse range of verbal and visual statements, from a few words scratched into a wall to commissioned murals under motorway flyovers. Identifying and naming the different manifestations can be problematic. Is graffiti fundamentally a form of writing and is stencil graffiti distinguished by its use of images? If so, how should we classify these four examples where much more painterly effects are incorporated into the words and images? Perceiving differences does not automatically bring with it the vocabulary needed to verbalise them.

Colloquial language | Language and difference | Language and popular print | Activity three | Summary

76

Illicit street 'gallery'
Bansky, 2006

The use of already familiar powerful images and stereotyped body language is part of the weaponry used by stencil graffitists to give immediate impact to their own message.

77

Railwayside graffiti
London 2006

Reading graffiti writing is much easier when you have begun to understand the codes and conventions. A dub or throwup is the writer's signature with an infill of white (or black), silver or gold.

78

Railwayside graffiti
London 2006

When more than two colours are
used the writing becomes a piece,
the more elaborate pieces becoming
a painting or masterpiece.

79

Railwayside graffiti
London 2006

This looks very like a 'go over', one
graffiti writer writing over another's
writing. If so, it is an example of the
competitive spirit among graffitists.

80

Railwayside graffiti
London 2006

Figurative images are far less
common in graffiti than letters and
words. This example is most
unusual in being entirely pictorial.
Its very faded, crumbling surface is
also a reminder that graffiti is
almost always short-lived, erased or
weathered away.

81

Newsagent's stand

The retailing of newspapers, magazines and journals is not restricted to newsagents but includes supermarkets, grocery stores, petrol stations and art galleries. And this does not include the ubiquitous free newspapers picked up in the street or pushed through the letter box. Even the smallest retail outlet is likely to stock at least ten newspapers with anything upward of 50 different magazines. The number of different kinds of magazines continues to increase, catering to the proliferation of interests and tastes in our consumer society. All are engaged in some way in the verbalising of the visual.

Language and popular print

Strictly speaking, a journal is a daily record. What it records can be diverse or very specialised in subject matter. It can be a very personal, intimate document or intended for a very wide readership, as are popular magazines and newspapers (*journal* and *giornale* are French and Italian for a newspaper). Worldwide, there are currently more printed newspapers and magazines than ever before, some of them of only minority interest. But popular newspapers and magazines presuppose a number of common characteristics: they address subjects and issues of common interest, suited to the tastes of ordinary people and written in an easily accessible, readerly language that does not need explanation. On occasions, however, the persistent use of very familiar words and concepts produces little more than a string of clichés. This is the negative aspect of journalism; journalese.

Within visual culture, there are a substantial number of specialist journals distributed worldwide, mostly targeted at peer-group professionals or students. They rarely, if at all, use the readily accessible language of popular journalism, but there are exceptions. Specialist journals by definition address current issues of concern to their readers. They are written by specialists for specialists and assume a high degree of familiarity with the vocabulary and concepts of the particular discipline. Academic journals are characterised by their academic language. It is mostly those journals addressed to a wider audience that depart from this very formal kind of writing. This is often the case with journals dealing with one or more areas of design. The current issues that concern the readers here go beyond the academic to include the practicalities of design, production and marketing.

Just as unfamiliar to the general public are the press releases and notices sent to journalists that constitute in themselves a specialised category of journalism. These are promotional journalism and part of a wider marketing strategy, as the often rhetorical language betrays. There is a liberal use of persuasive adjectives: exhibitions are major, books are seminal. But they can provide necessary factual information, usually stating what and how many items will be exhibited, or indicate the curatorial point of view as in the ubiquitous, 'The exhibition will examine…(or investigate)'. On occasions, they can even offer in advance of anyone seeing the exhibition or reading the book a brief analysis and evaluation. In these several ways, the aim is to put the viewer or reader in a receptive frame of mind. Much the same kind of language is used in exhibition guides available to the general public and for much the same purpose.

Both press releases and exhibition guides are, in effect, previews just like the preview briefings or feature-length pieces in newspapers and magazines, of which the following is an example:

'(Bill) Viola creates poetic symbols of our existence using the cold detachment of a video camera. His new exhibition is based on Wagner's opera *Tristan und Isolde*, in which he recounts the lovers' journey through death and liberation, offering a spine-chilling allegory of these turbulent modern times.'
Guardian, The Guide, 17–23 June, 2006
Not all previews are as rhetorical and emotive as this but all attempt the impossible task of summarising in words an all-embracing experience. There are valuable lessons to be learned here for students engaged in verbalising the visual, not least the need to choose the right kind of language for the given occasion.

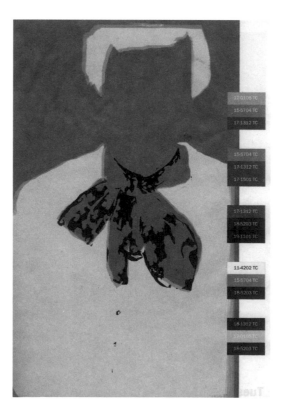

82

**Textile View magazine
issue 73, spring 2006**

The specialist quarterly, *Textile View Magazine* uses the accessible text of popular journalism. Language Such as:

'Summer 2007 is a timeless season where colours bloom and put rhythm into our silhouettes'

is not academic any more than:

'Dictates of beauty are no longer imposed but rise from our creative impulses, allowing us to invent our fineries and decors.'

The context for these statements is that of colour prediction for the coming year in fashion and, therefore, addressed to those in the fashion textile industry. The primary aim is to create a particular mood, much like the panels of images, shapes, colours and textures assembled by designers.

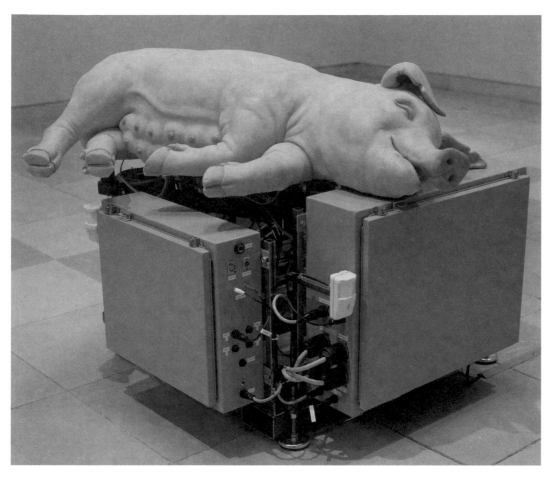

Mechanical Pig
Paul McCarthy, 2005

'American artist Paul McCarthy is one of the most influential artists of his generation. Revealing the darker side of American and European myths, his work transforms popular icons from Pinocchio to Santa Claus into disturbing, carnivalesque scenarios'.

Whitechapel Art Gallery, London, *Gallery Guide*, 23 October 2005–8 January, 2006.

Analytical, critically evaluative and interpretative, this paragraph exemplifies the persuasive language used by journalists to put the exhibition visitor into a receptive frame of mind.

Star Star
Jason Fox, 2006

'Often the central focus for Fox's paintings are hybrid creations of fictionalised misfits, heroes or antiheroes and the works can be referenced to art visionaries such as Goya and Picasso and to genres such as science fiction, blax-ploitation films and video game iconography.'

Alexandre Pollazzon Ltd. Gallery, London, Press Release for Jason Fox exhibition 2 June–8 July 2006

The similarities between this statement and the one accompanying the Paul McCarthy image are obvious although one is for general public consumption and the other directed at art critics.

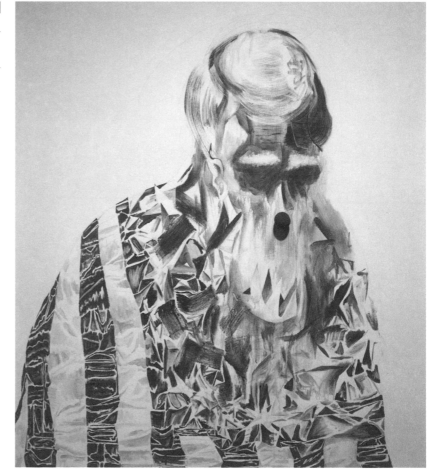

Colloquial language   Language and difference   Language and popular print   Activity three   Summary

Magazines

Although in practice there may be little to distinguish some journals from magazines given their common concerns with particular subject areas and, therefore, a particular group of readers, the connotations of each are different. Quarterly journals are much more closely associated with academia, as the kind of language they use often clearly indicates. Monthly magazines generally have a wider appeal, some of them with circulation figures sufficient to be called popular. The language used is, usually, if not always, of an accessible, even colloquial kind. In general, the narrower the focus of the magazine, the more specialised the vocabulary and concepts employed.

i-D magazine is primarily a magazine of the visual arts but as its title suggests, its range is sufficiently broad to be categorised as a life-style publication. The writing is serious and informed but the overall tone is closer to conversation than a postgraduate thesis. For example:

'The Milan Furniture Fair presents a vast spectacle each April of design colliding with commerce. Two million feet of exhibition space, plus more than 300 offsite venues, turn the city into a galaxy of sparkling concepts. Some will achieve durability as products, a few immortality; many will flame out.'

Editorial, i-D magazine, June 2006

This is rhetorical if colloquial language, for example, 'a galaxy of sparkling concepts,' including slang, 'flame out', but it is representative of i-D and many other monthlies.

The language of magazine journalism is generally eclectic, incorporating words and phrases already familiar to and well-understood by the target group readers. These are mixed and matched according to the needs of the occasion. Formal and informal language can appear side by side in the same sentence, the occasional challenging concept made more accessible by descriptive writing that directly appeals to the senses. Illustrations with explanatory captions serve to arrest attention and lead the reader into the more demanding text.

Where academic journals with their few, if any, illustrations implicitly assume the reader is familiar with the relevant images, magazines offer a much more integrated experience. The difficult task of verbalising the visual is made easier where the reader sees the images. Words and images are brought into a closer working relationship. Over the last two decades or so, the advantages of this greater integration of the verbal and the visual have been recognised increasingly by publishers of academic histories of art. The time when scholarly books had their texts first and a few rather dull, monochrome images at the back have passed. Integrating images and text and placing the images within the text has now become accepted practice for student essays and dissertations.

Airstream trailer, 2006

Commenting on the Airstream Trailer, *Blueprint* magazine (April, 2006) wrote:

'Put away your driving gloves and hide the doilies, the Airstream trailer – the curvy retro king of the US highway – is coming to a road near you'.

This mimics the language patterns of popular cinema commercials. Yet this very informal kind of writing does not exclude awareness of the Airstream's Modernist status.

The industrial design historian, John Heskett, wrote of the original 1931 Airstream trailer that it:

'vehemently asserted its modernity, its gleaming organic form becoming a cult object.'
John Heskett, *Industrial Design*, Thames & Hudson, 1980.

Blueprint's gloss on this is:

'The Airstream has always been a cult item among architects.'

Design history and design journalism sometimes share the same language.

Mexico '68 logo
Lance Wyman, 1968

Creative Review magazine claims in its subtitle to be 'The Best in Visual Communication', so it is no surprise to discover a feature (June 2006) on Lance Wyman, the graphic designer of the 1968 logo for the Olympic Games in Mexico City. The language here, however, can at times seem much closer to the elevated, specialist vocabulary of formal design writing but often with intrusions from the vernacular that puncture any possibility of the pretentious, as in, 'His is work that relies on the interpretation of spatial, cultural and visual context, instead of relying on the advances of printing and digital technologies to create immediate wow-factor.' Read out of context, the 'wow-factor' would alert any attentive reader to the likelihood of this being a piece of journalism rather than academic design writing.

Trilogy part 2
Daniel Gustav Cramer, 2006

Dazed and Confused magazine's appeal is decidedly to those in their late teens and twenties, perhaps mostly students, but definitely not with conventional tastes. Unlike many other monthlies directed at a teen-twenties readership, it regularly reviews fine art and design. The writing is informed but casually so, the contextualising references and allusions those most familiar to an undergraduate readership. Eva Wiseman's review of the Cramer exhibition of photographs (March 2006) responded vividly to the connotations of the images, supporting these with appropriate statements made by the artist:

'In Daniel Cramer's photographs, a once romantic landscape becomes an eerie forest – the scene set for red-hooded girls to be eaten, and for sweet-toothed twins to be snatched.'

On first reading at least, not everyone would relate 'red-hooded girls' to Little Red Riding Hood or 'sweet-toothed twins' to Hansel and Gretel. Here, Wiseman leaves the reader to recognise the references and allusions she makes, which is an indication of the kind of person who regularly reads *Dazed and Confused*.

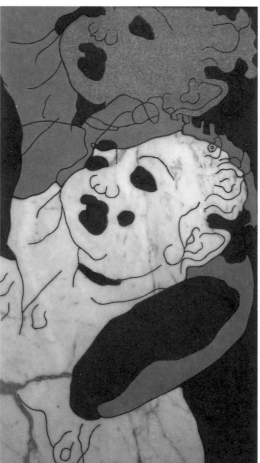

The Twins
Gary Hume, 2006

In terms of language and the way that metaphors, visual references and connotations can conjure up the experience of a single artefact or entire exhibition, a freebie newspaper, the London *Metro*, can readily be compared with *Dazed and Confused*. Reviewing a Gary Hume exhibition of paintings (*Metro*, May 30 2006), Fisun Guner wrote:

'From ordinary, yelping sprogs swaddled in all-in-ones, to plump putti, those winged cherubs of the Renaissance, floating on decorative backdrops, Hume has embraced the subject with the Baroque exuberance of an artist confident enough to enjoy risk.'

Crucially, here 'plump putti', if not 'Baroque exuberance', are explained to the reader. Fisun Guner's review of Hume's exhibition says much about the core imagery and surface effects of the paintings, but without the illustration, would readers expect the pictures to be as they are?

Popular print and fine art

Popular publications do not necessarily have massive circulations. Some are popular among quite small groups. No national newspaper has equal appeal for everybody. Some large-circulation newspapers do not engage with fine art, unless the subject has given rise to wide public concern. The newspaper then might use all its rhetorical powers to persuade its readers to adopt a particular opinion.

The most popular and numerous magazines dealing with fine art are those targeted on the amateur, typically someone who goes to exhibitions and also practises in their spare time one or another of the visual arts but is not academically oriented. Instructive articles on materials and techniques are common. But although there is usually a very clear emphasis upon traditional representational art, the content of these magazines does not exclude the occasional article on one or another early 20th century avant-garde artist or movement or even some commentary on more recent developments, especially if these have attracted the attention of the popular press. The language is always conversational, even ingratiatingly so, the reader often directly addressed as 'you' and this personalising approach is reinforced by the number of biographical articles on or even interviews with practising artists. This collusive approach is less evident in other monthly magazines that deal with the visual arts but it can be identified.

Other magazines concerned with fine art are addressed to other subcultural groups. Some of these magazines have a very small circulation and, being available only in specialist retail outlets or online, are unknown to the wider public. Perhaps not surprisingly, in the language and overall layout of their printed editions these can resemble zines possibly because they too rely upon DIY modes of production or share a similar aesthetic. As a general rule, the larger the circulation the more professional the standards of publication. The overall look of a widely distributed monthly magazine directed at a teen to twenties readership may not conform to standard practice but the level of execution will.

Popular print and design

Unlike fine art, photography and or even architecture, most newspapers, including the so-called serious ones, do not regularly review or write about design, which is surprising for it is by far the most commonly experienced category within visual culture and might be expected to occupy centre-stage. Where there is some interest, the two most common design subjects addressed in newspapers, although most likely relegated to their magazine or supplementary sections, are fashion and interior decoration, where the language is least likely to resemble that of formal historical, theoretical or critical writing on the same subjects.

In Western culture, the long tradition of writing on architecture with its specialised theoretical and technical language and its established canon of great architects and buildings is not paralleled in other areas of design. The explanation is not difficult to find. In the West, there is a decisive division between fine and applied art. Architecture was very early set beside painting, sculpture, literature and music as a fine art form, despite its evident functional utility. Many other cultures do not have this hierarchical division in which a piece of sculpture is judged more significant than a salt cellar. That is unless the salt cellar be designed, if not made, by an esteemed sculptor like Benvenuto Cellini, in which case the language used to discuss the object is that used to discuss works of sculpture, not a utilitarian object. In other cultures there is far less distinction made between the significance of a scroll painting, a screen or a garden pavilion.

Regular writing on fashion has existed in Europe from at least the 18th century but the language employed did not acquire an equivalent level of specialised accuracy to that of architecture until much later, unless it be that of technical terms. In general, regular writing on design emerges along with Modernism and very closely linked to the Industrial Revolution and the development of mass production. This has partly determined the kind of vocabulary and concepts used and the influence of this early language can be identified in much contemporary writing on design. Many of the terms used to characterise postmodern design, such as ornamental, hybrid or pastiche depend for their full significance on their Modernist, binary opposites, functional, unitary and authentic. Newspapers and popular magazines rely upon elements of this vocabulary, especially when they want their text to have a credible authority.

TOP TIP BAN BRASH BANANA YELLOWS IN FAVOUR OF SAFFRONS AND OCHRES, BUT AVOID BLANKET COLOUR AND LAYER DIFFERENT TONES FOR BALANCE AND DEPTH

89

**Page from Elle Decoration
July 2006**

In a feature article on colour in the home in *Elle Decoration* magazine (July 2006), readers are advised that:

'The first thing to remember is that yellow is essentially an attention-grabbing hue, which means it should only be used in areas you really want to highlight: think feature walls, sexy surfaces and centre pieces. Ayurvedic therapists and colour-theorists point to yellow's associations with food, happiness, confidence and intellect, which means it's ideal for dining areas, social spaces and home offices.'

Colloquialisms such as, 'it's', 'attention-grabbing' and 'sexy surfaces' aside, it is worth comparing this statement on colour with that by Kandinsky. Semantically, they may have more in common than one might expect.

Wind turbine

Reporting on the development of a new wind turbine, the *Guardian* newspaper's environmental editor, John Vidal, (2 June 2006) wrote:

'Wind turbines are tall white objects with three long blades and they sit on hilltops spinning around to generate electricity, right? Wrong.' The report concludes that, 'Not only do turbines generate electricity; they can double up as art or even advertising hoardings.'

Compared with fine art reviews, this is very sober, denotative language but it has its tropes (figure of speech). To 'sit' on a hillside in this context is metaphoric, possibly anthropomorphic. The question, 'right?' is rhetorical, one asked for effect rather than relying upon an answer, which in this case is promptly given anyway. The concluding sentence is speculative, but the affirmative 'can', is used instead of 'might'.

De la Warr Pavilion, Bexhill-on-Sea
Erich Mendelsohn and
Serge Chermayeff, 1935–36

'Britain has few examples of top-flight modernism. The De la Warr Pavilion is definitely one…a public entertainment centre, a seafront pleasure palace in glass and glinting steel.… Beyond their rather daunting manifesto-speak, the modernists believed in having a good time.'
Fiona MacCarthy, *Guardian G2*, 20 March 2006.

Within the context of a newspaper article listing ten unmissable sights of Modernist architecture, MacCarthy manages in very few words to judge the British contribution and, through a carefully calculated use of adjectives and nouns, 'seafront pleasure palace', 'glinting', turn the prescriptive austerities of Modernist theory upside down. Writing from a postmodern perspective, MacCarthy can use the terms of Postmodernism to re-evaluate a Modernist building.

Activity three
How well do reviews communicate?

Che Guevara: revolutionary and icon.
Victoria and Albert Museum, London,
6 June–28 August, 2006

Read the four (edited) previews and reviews on
the facing page, and then, using the following
questions, try to evaluate how well each one
communicates some sense of both
experiencing and appreciating the exhibition.

1   Is the central purpose of the exhibition clearly
    communicated?

2   Is the subject of the exhibition placed in its
    historical and cultural context?

3   To what extent is the success of the central
    purpose of the exhibition critically evaluated?

4   What kind of language does each preview or
    review employ?

92

Guerrillero Heroico
Alexander Korda, 1960

Alan Rutter
Time Out, London
31 May–7 June 2006

'There was a time when Camden (London) was communist – or at least it looked that way. On a stroll up the lock, you'd be bombarded with images on badges, T-shirts and posters of romantic Red revolutionary Che Guevara…and the image was always the same one: a single frame captured by one Alberto Korda. The powerful image…became a rallying symbol for protestors worldwide, from the student uprisings in Prague in 1968, through the Zapatistas in Mexico, to the Middle East today – appearing on posters, banners and murals…. For others, it's become a generic statement of romanticised, anti-establishment views…. More recently, its ubiquity has opened it up to pastiche and parody…. It is ironic that this Marxist revolutionary has probably helped shift more T-shirts, baseball caps and assorted tat than Mickey Mouse…. Korda's photograph and the mythology of Guevara go hand in hand.'

Richard Gott
Guardian Review
3 June 2006

'The famous photograph of Che Guevara snapped by Alberto Korda in 1960 has circulated through the globe in the past half century, endlessly reproduced in increasingly exotic forms, each created with different intentions and evoking varied responses…a new exhibition…concentrates specifically on the history and legacy of the Korda portrait, often known as the Guerrillero Heroico, the startling image with eyes gazing fiercely into some distant horizon, traditionally displayed in students' rooms…. Most of those who sport the Che Guevara logo today forget that he was the Osama bin Laden of his time…. Securely insulated from politics, Guevara's image is now largely perceived as a fashion accessory, the logo on the celebrity T-shirt or handbag…Korda…worked as a young man as a fashion photographer…. He aimed to be the Richard Avedon of Cuba. Taken by surprise by the guerrilla victory of 1959, he worked subsequently with Raul Corrales, Castro's official photographer, to capture the excitement of the revolution. In his image of Che, something survives of his earliest experience with beautiful women. With the extraordinarily long hair and wispy beard, it is a strikingly androgynous portrait, and in the 1970s it inevitably appeared on a poster as "Che Gay".'

Fiona Macdonald
London
6 June 2006

'It's the face that not so launched a thousand ships as provided the backdrop for student digs. The photograph of Ernesto "Che" Guevara taken by Alberto Korda on March 5, 1960 is thought to be the most reproduced image in the history of photography, and its many manifestations form the basis for the…exhibition…. Despite representing rebellion for millions of people since the Latin American revolutionary leader was snapped at a funeral cortege in Cuba, the portrait has also taken on a range of different meanings by its co-option unto advertising and merchandising.'

Peter Conrad
Observer
11 June 2006

'The fate of a single image, documented in a concise and clever exhibition at the V&A, sums up our lapse from idealism to the plump, smug hoarding of our material gains. In 1960 the photographer Alberto Korda snapped Che Guevara at a rally in Cuba – shag-haired, frowning with messianic intensity, and wearing his zip-up leather jacket as if it were a clerical soutane, the uniform of his fanatical creed. Korda called the image Guerrillero Heroico, allegorised Che…. After Che's assination in 1967, Korda's portrait – now starkly simplified, with beret lifting off to form a halo and its red star holding out a remote hope that heaven might still be established on Earth – found its way on to posters, lapel badges and T-shirts. It became a testament to martyrdom, and the tragic souvenir of a lost cause…. The image persists, but these days it has a different meaning. The enemy of capitalism has been co-opted, and killed over again; the freedom fighter, transformed into a commercial brand, now greases transactions in the consumer economy and sells opium to the masses.'

93

Cher Guevara
Scott King, 2001

94

GuevIRA, 1993

Summary

1

English language still maintains a distinction between what is said (colloquial) and what is written (formal, academic).

2

English, although now universally prioritised, is not a universal language.

3

The distinction between formal and informal language in English is probably etymological; ancient Greek and Latin for formal language and Germanic or Anglo-Saxon for informal.

4

Anglophone culture, just like any other, is not a unified language; sub-cultural differences prevail.

7

Translated language is always a compromise between the particularities of the original language and those of the language into which the original is translated.

10

Journalistic writing is usually immediately accessible, presupposing no need for further interpretation of the information given in the text.

5

The language most suited to discussing a visual culture such as graffiti is not appropriate to discussing Italian Renaissance painting and sculpture.

8

The language of journalism is not unified but reflective of the vocabulary and concepts of its target readership.

6

Colloquial language can be no less particular and exclusive than formal, academic language. Both are acquired language patterns.

9

Journalism is most often eclectic in the choice of language, mixing and matching according the occasion.

04 Studio talk

04

Studio talk

95

Two audio cassettes
Giulio Miglietta, 2006

The left-hand cassette was drawn
with the student's usual right hand
and the right-hand one with his left.
Both were drawn within only a few
minutes, and neither drawing
qualifies as a carefully considered
example of academic
draughtsmanship. There are
parallels to be drawn here with oral
statements. Unlike the considered,
carefully worded written statement,
oral communication, especially
everyday speech, is spontaneous,
characterised by abbreviations,
elisions and omissions. An audio
cassette is one medium for
recording these characteristics,
including tone of voice, accent
and emphases.

Language and oral communication

In spoken language, the pitch of the voice, accent, emphases, enunciation and pronunciation are as important as the choice of words in conveying meaning. Printed dialogue can give some sense of this: punctuation can indicate phrasing or even an exclamatory statement; italicising words can indicate emphases. 'It is a *good* picture' and 'It is a good picture!' are examples. But the overall tone of the voice with its multitudinous inflections is lost. Maybe that is why spoken language has so often been prioritised over written language. It is claimed to be more authentic, possessing greater authority. The presence of the speaker has its advantages. Yet speech has its limitations. Unlike the reader who can re-read a statement if it is not understood the first time, the listener has only the one occasion. Hearing clearly and understanding immediately are vital.

Conversation

Much of our daily conversation falls far short of the recommended ideals of clarity and precision in good verbal communication. We fail to complete sentences altogether or rely upon the listener to do it for us as in, 'and so on', 'do you get me?' or 'see what I mean?'. We frequently speak in phrases, but deliver them as if they were sentences with finite verbs.

Members of a peer or subcultural group usually understand each other sufficiently to enable incomplete sentences and fragmentary phrases to communicate satisfactorily. The speaker is assuming other members of the group are so informed about the subject being addressed that they can complete the undeclared end of the sentence or phrase, as the examples above show.

But conversational language patterns go beyond any particular group. Elisions are ubiquitous, as in, 'aren't they?', 'don't you think?', 'I've done this'. Interjections, such as, 'really?', 'wow!', or, 'cool' are almost as numerous. There are also those innumerable, repetitious habits of speech. Some are personal, the favoured vocabulary of the speaker, as in, for example, the consistent use of 'marvellous' rather than 'wonderful' or an equivalent. Others are part of the collective language of a culture. Repeatedly beginning a sentence, sometimes inappropriately, with 'basically' is a typical example, as is the use of 'like' in 'So I thought like…', meaning 'So I thought that…'. Consideration of the specific language to be used for a particular audience is important if communication is to be ensured.

Dialogue

In group discussions, statements are made, the audience receives and interprets the statements and responds. This is dialogue; a verbal interchange of thoughts, opinions or feelings. The entire group may agree with any one or all the statements made but not always. Questions may be asked. An original statement may be challenged by one of the group making a contrary statement. And so the chain of communication continues. Whether or not the discussion reaches an agreed conclusion, the literary parallel here is drama, with its progressive exchange of differing points of view, not the novel, where a single narrative voice usually dominates.

The dialogue will ideally reflect the diversity of knowledge and experience that each student brings to any group discussion, but the dialogue has to be conducted within a broadly agreed pattern of language, especially specialist language. For students of visual culture, this means acquiring as soon as possible a firm hold on the meaning and use of the vocabulary and concepts widely employed in any serious discourse on art and design in any given language. This is not easy, but once acquired, the benefits become increasingly clear in terms of both accuracy and confidence.

The studio discussion of one student's Christmas vacation design assignment, 'Pocket Monet' (a pun on 'pocket money'), is typical of very many. The names of several famous, international people had been randomly distributed as subjects among the group, the design requirement being something that epitomised the subject but small enough to go into a pocket. This particular student was given the Turkish nation-builder and nationalist leader, Mustafa Kemal Ataturk.

Asked by the tutor, 'Have you finished it?' she replied, 'Yes, but my friend was messing around. The thing is I couldn't use the double-sided printer thing so I just cut and stuck it up.' When the tutor then asked if she or anyone in the group had heard of Ataturk before, the answer was no but the student continued, 'Obviously I'm gonna examine his life.… At Christmas, I got a book on astrology so basically looked his birthday up. First of March so he was Pisces (the fish sign). I made a connection between that and events in Turkey.'

As the discussion focused on the design work, one participant asked, 'What about the fish?' adding 'I wouldn't have known about astrology and Pisces.' The student explained, 'A school of fish is like people following him'.

96

Turkish banknote

A current Turkish banknote was the base material for a number of interventionist additions and modifications by the student.

97

Pocket Monet
Keisha Ferrell, 2005

The choice of the banknote was generally approved. The observation of a fellow student, 'Money is powerful and he was a powerful person,' summing this up.

98a

98b

Pocket Monet
Keisha Ferrell, 2005

'Visually, I think it works,' was a common response among fellow students but there were reservations. 'You've layered it with so much,' leading to: 'Needs some editing.'

Monologue

If possible, it is always advisable to ascertain what kind of language is appropriate to any oral presentation if communication is to be successful. Even within a relatively contained peer group like that of first-year undergraduates all on the same course of study, it is unwise to assume too high a degree of common understanding. All too likely, the group will contain students from quite different cultural backgrounds, each bringing their own expectations and patterns of understanding. Differences in understanding and interpretation are inevitable even among students from the same language culture and widen where the group contains students from quite different language cultures.
In the 1930s, C. K. Ogden developed what he called Basic English, reducing the vast vocabulary of the language to 850 words. Although this is no longer generally employed, it is easily paralleled today in what professional interpreters of other languages into English would recognise as International English: a basic vocabulary that is readily understood by very many others using English as a second language. Within the context of any specialist discipline, this includes the relevant specialist language. Anyone addressing an international audience in whatever language might consider reducing their vocabulary to the most familiar and, therefore, readily understood.

Talking about the gestation and development of a still unfinished work can be hazardous for many, the inconclusiveness of the material being dealt with too amorphous to describe. This was the case in the early stages of a typographic assignment, 'Word'. The task was to use a variety of methods to record conversations using only type, but taking into consideration how all the senses are affected by the circumstances; in other words, synaesthetic experience.

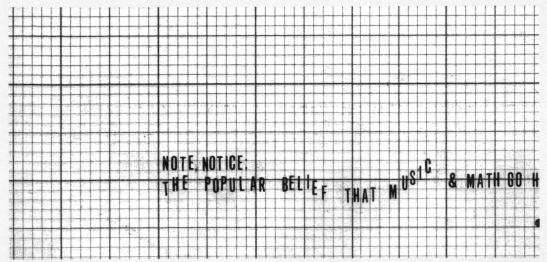

Graph paper abstract
Sara Colding, 2005

Parallelling the student's oral presentation, this is one tentative attempt at a solution to the assignment brief; trying to find visual equivalents to the rise and fall of the spoken words.

The student began falteringly, 'I don't know. What would it feel like? Just really doing drawings…. Just like sort of mirroring how I feel inside. I didn't know what to do,' but gained confidence when a possible solution presented itself. 'Then I had this dream with three different 'wes'. Well it was pretty scary but it was kind of fun as well. I decided to use that one. All these different wes talking to each other, saying different things.'

Uncertainty returned with the exploration of this idea, 'I looked at some dream dictionaries for inspiration then poetry and architecture and line drawings and rhythm and second-hand books for conversations and words and bits of type and layouts. And there's this thing in Sweden called something like maiden novels, like cheap romantic novels…. Looked into that and stuff, things like this, personal dedications and notes by readers. Didn't know where to go from there, actually. Nothing really happened…. Just wanted something I could work on initially.'

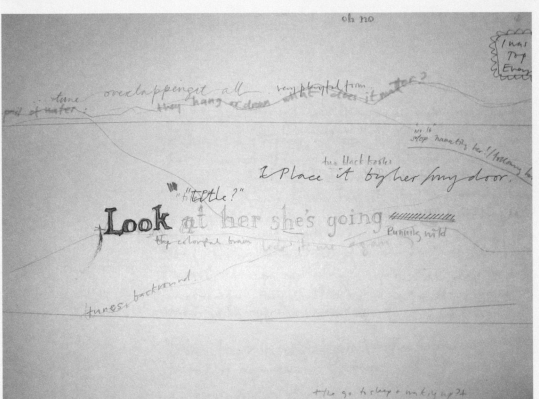

100

Look At Her
Sara Colding, 2005

These sketchbook notations are exploratory, testing possibilities rather than arriving at a conclusion. They mirror the hesitancy of the oral account.

Double-page exploration
Lakweena Suit, 2005

A sketchbook example that visually parallels the design development verbalised in the oral presentation.

Recollecting all the stages of a design assignment after its completion has the advantage of hindsight. Choices have been made, uncertainties resolved, the progressive thread inviting a chronological, narrative account. Another student recalling her experiences on the same 'Word' assignment seized the opportunity. 'I looked at Martin Luther King and lots of stuff he did. The civil rights thing. There was the boycotting of the buses in Montgomery, Alabama, and I found information about that.

I found this conversation with an old lady. "The spirit of the protest had so become a part of people's lives that sometimes they preferred to walk when a ride was available. Once a poor driver stopped beside an elderly woman trudging along with obvious difficulties. 'Jump on, grandmother,' he said, 'You don't need to walk.' She waved him on. 'I am not walking for myself. I am walking for my children and grandchildren.'" It really touched me...the power in that, the whole image of her laying herself down so that future generations would be raised up.'

Red Type statement
Lakweena Suit, 2005

One possible solution, ultimately rejected, was to remove all traces of the personal and have the type mimic the self-effacing statement of the black woman.

'I came up with the idea here of taking out anything personal... because it's not a personal feeling it's just sacrificing herself. Then I became really confused...had another brainstorm, going back to basics, seeing ways of writing down this real conversation.... I came up with the idea instead of taking out anything personal just taking out the "Is"... I would have a number of conversations like here and as the conversations go along the "Is" get lower and lower because she is laying herself down for the cause.'

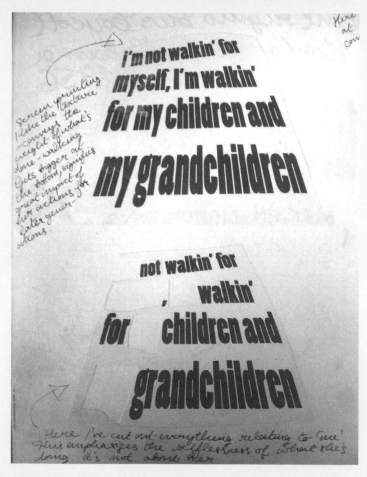

04 Studio talk

AM NOT WALKIN FOR MYSELF I AM WALKIN FOR MY CHILDREN AND MY GRANDCHILDREN

AM NOT WALKIN FOR MYSELF I AM WALKIN FOR MY CHILDREN AND MY GRANDCHILDREN

'AM NOT WALKIN FOR MYSELF I AM WALKIN FOR MY CHILDREN AND MY GRANDCHILDREN

AM NOT WALKIN FOR MYSELF I AM WALKIN FOR MY CHILDREN AND MY GRANDCHILDREN

AM NOT WALKIN FOR MYSELF I AM WALKIN FOR MY CHILDREN AND MY GRANDCHILDREN

AM NOT WALKIN FOR MYSELF I AM WALKIN FOR MY CHILDREN AND MY GRANDCHILDREN

AM NOT WALKIN FOR MYSELF I AM WALKIN FOR MY CHILDREN AND MY GRANDCHILDREN

Final Image
Lakweena Suit, 2005

This is the final realisation of the Montgomery black woman's statement.

'Then I looked at the text.… She is an old woman so needs to have a weak text to convey the struggle… but I realised, listening to the freedom songs…what she was doing was not actually so…sure she was struggling physically…but inside, the message of what she was doing was such a strong bold message that I didn't want a frail, weak writing. So I looked at this writing by Neville Brody.… It's a little higgledy-piggledy, a bit wonky, but it is something strong.…I thought for the children and grandchildren what I'd do.…The "I" would be raised up as time went on…and at the end they are standing up. She has been laid down but they are standing up.… It's like a ticking clock so it represents the time of what is happening.'

Like any conventional story, this second account has a definite beginning, middle and end and in that order.

This word project, set within the context of typographical design, demonstrates the search for a solution that would resolve the relationship between the meanings of the words used and their visualisation. This was as much a central concern for this student as was her commitment to the chosen subject. Her oral presentation was in many ways exemplary. With unusually detailed information on the research, design development, evaluation and final realisation of the project, every significant stage in the progression of the assignment is addressed. The language is consistently colloquial, the sequencing and pace of the delivery creating considerable momentum in the presentation.

Interview

Unlike group discussions where all the participants help determine the direction of the dialogue, an interview is fundamentally interrogative, a question and answer structure in which the interviewer is largely responsible for the questions put to the interviewee. Sometimes the questions can be rigidly predetermined. On other occasions they arise from the responding statements of the interviewee, as in the interview recorded here. An interview is, of course, a kind of dialogue but a restricted one both in the number of participants and the possible control exercised by the interviewer. Ideally, it is an equal, reciprocal relationship, a face to face encounter for the purpose of consultation, but it can also be an interrogation of someone suspected of a misdemeanour. An interview, therefore, can be more threatening than either a monologue or a dialogue. The interviewee must be attentive to all the connotations of the questions put to them and the implications of their answers. Vigilance is required if the interviewee is to exercise control over the direction of the interview. Students might find themselves in either of these roles, interviewer or interviewee, and need to be prepared for both.

In almost all cases, however, whether the student is interviewing or being interviewed, the situation is for the most part a reciprocal one. The language employed by the participants can vary considerably according to the speakers; almost exclusively formal–academic, informal–colloquial or, more likely, a mixture of both. A single example of an interview cannot be made representative of all these factors but it can illustrate a number of frequently encountered contexts in which the questions put to the interviewee are satisfactorily answered. The example used here immediately establishes the degree to which students, from the beginning of the assignment, was consciously pursuing the potential of her chosen subject and how different and accessible and always approriate to the context. All the questions are answered, the information given repeatedly going beyond that required and indicating the extent to which the interviewee was as much in control as the interviewer.

Errata

p. 126, line 13: The example used here immediately establishes the degree to which students, from the beginning of the assignment, was consciously pursuing the potential of her chosen subject and how different and accessible and always appropriate to the context.

This should read: The example used here immediately establishes the degree to which the student, from the beginning of the assignment, was consciously pursuing the potential of her chosen subject and how the different possibilities might contribute to the final outcome, in this case a book. The language used is clear, readily accessible and always appropriate to the context.

The assignment, *Headlines Give Me Headaches When I Read Them,* required the student to read a local newspaper and select one article/story for an in-depth investigation. The student interviewed here chose a piece announcing a charity balloon race that was to be started by an Olympic medal-winning runner. The interview took place after completion of the assignment.

What was your first response to the brief and why did you choose your article?

I was looking for an article that had scope to be interesting and be developed. I was looking for a bit of an angle. It was about a balloon race so there was an actual event I could attend and take photographs and we were encouraged to get primary and secondary evidence so it would be an ideal opportunity.... It would be interesting visually because of the balloon race and everything that entailed and because there was a charity behind it we had the kind of background information for a book.

So this gave a wider social dimension to the task?

Yes...there was a substance to it and an opportunity to produce a book about a charity that people might not know.

Who did you interview?

I interviewed...a press officer from the charity...and then on the actual day, I interviewed all the people who were helping with the balloon race and I spoke to some volunteers from Sense. There were press photographers there and the celebrity.

Did you have any communication with the press?

We were all bundled together and they were professionals.... When I turned up with my camera they all just assumed I was the press and I said no, I was just a student from university. They let me stand with their officer. There was a professional photographer for Sense...I had to stand next to the star so I never got a straight-on shot of him. But no, it was fun.

What were you trying to investigate?

There were a couple of angles I wanted to look at. The actual event itself...the charity, Sense, which is for deaf-blindness...I researched deaf-blindness, the kinds of diseases that cause it, and so I widened it from the initial event.

Who did you expect to be interested in the research you carried out?

Realistically, it was done for the sake of the book...but there are people who are interested in the charity, interested in fund-raising, also people who may know about Sense but not what the charity does or might not have really considered deaf-blindness because really it is very specific: it's not just deafness or blindness.... A few people might be interested because they didn't know about it. Obviously, it wasn't going to be put out in the public ground!

Would you say your primary concern was raising awareness, giving information, or a combination of both?

I guess it was a combination.... There was no point in just focusing on the event. That is why I developed it into other sections.

What would you estimate to be the benefits of having done this assignment?

It made me go out and get primary evidence, to actually speak to the guy at Sense. To go to the event forced me to speak to the people there. Because I interacted with them, I found a little bit of personal history for each of them, their different reasons for being there.... Just seeing the pictures on their website...I wouldn't have known the gas cylinders arrived late and they had problems with the balloons.... In a way it maybe gives you more of an emphasis to put that story across.

**The Balloon Race: In the Bag 200
Alexis Mutkin, 2005**

'I think it is quite methodical in that
I start at the beginning where the
balloons are just in the bag.... I just
documented their filling up.'

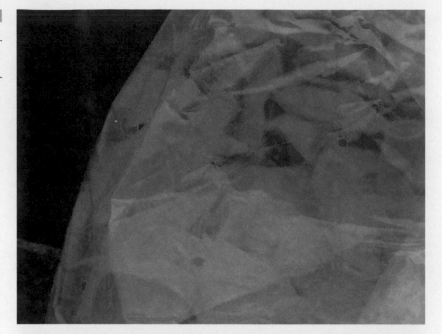

105

**The Balloon Race: Getting Ready
Alexis Mutkin, 2005**

'I kind of progress on to them
getting the event ready in a more or
less chronological order.... The
images record the development of
the event.'

106

**The Balloon Race: the Release
Alexis Mutkin, 2005**

'The images of the balloons give a
sense of the build up...and it ends
with their release. They're off!'

107

Oral Presentation

Live oral presentations go beyond the aural. A careful targeting of the audience, consideration of the kind of language used, a measured pacing in the delivery, all contribute to effective communication. But as this photograph shows, facial and body language can be just as important as verbal language.
An oral presentation is a physical performance too.

Oral presentations

Although still a spoken delivery, formal oral presentations, that is, those prepared in advance, presume a much more formal kind of language than the everyday speech used in spontaneous monologues and dialogues about art and design work. Students called upon to make an oral presentation are given time to consider the subject, carry out appropriate research and organise the material in advance. Organising the material to fit the time allowed is a crucial requirement. Structuring the material to suit the conditions is crucial.

Addressing the audience

Clear enunciation and pronunciation using standard diction are generally recommended. These considerations are made even more important when the presentation is given to students from different language cultures and possibly with only a limited experience of the one being used by the speaker. Making a correct assessment of the audience in terms of age, cultural background, language ability and familiarity with the subject is a major factor in any successful presentation, as is the choice of visual or other supporting material and how it is integrated with the oral.

Rather than speaking from a few bullet points listing the essential items to be addressed, some students, made nervous by the prospect of standing up in front of an audience, are tempted to write out in full what they intend to say then either learn it by heart or read it out. A student with appropriate performing skills like those of a good actor might succeed with the first option. The second is invariably a recipe for failure. Speed of delivery, pacing and pausing are necessary if the audience is to receive and properly understand what is said. Reading almost always results in a too regularised rhythm and monotonous effect. Because oral presentations are by definition spoken ones, some of the characteristics of ordinary speech, such as elisions, a hesitant or occasionally faltering delivery, are entirely acceptable, even contributing to the desirable variety. They are widely accepted as the signs of authenticity, the authorial voice of the speaker.

Short oral presentations: a sample

The following four presentations were made by a group of international students from different specialist design subject areas in response to a common assignment. The year one undergraduate programme of lectures and seminars for the term was an examination of Postmodernism and the assignment asked students to prepare and present a five-minute oral presentation to their peer group using a single artefact to illustrate their definition of the difficult and contested concept, Postmodernism. Because all the students had attended the same programme, assessing the audience was relatively easy.

Unlike the preceding examples of studio talk, here the students were not dealing with their own or a fellow student's work but artefacts written, designed, directed and produced by professionals and considered within the context of history and theory as well as practice. The need to provide essential information, identify key issues and support a particular point of view with appropriate evidence had been clearly recognised. But the choice of subject, manner of presentation and kind of language used varied considerably yet without any significant differences in overall achievement.

108

----

iPod user

'Postmodernism promotes parody...all those people walking around in their own bubble of private space, with white wires trailing from their ears.'

109

----

iPod Nano displayed on an Apple Powerbook

'Postmodernism embraces constant change and the various iSkins and covers you can now get for the iPod reflect this constant change, along with the various new formats such as the Nano (illustrated here), Photo and Video iPods.'

110

Apple Powerbook screen, iMusic library

'Postmodernism argues that copies are as good as originals and...the digital music and videos that iPods play is exactly the same as the original, because digital copying does not change or lose information.'

Presentation one

Perhaps the most informal of the presentations, including the ubiquitous 'basically', was this one on the iPod. The colloquial language ('Postmodernism argues that copies are as good as originals,' used in preference to Jean Baudrillard's theoretical concepts, simulacra and simulation) and personalised approach ('I don't know much about philosophy but from my research it's fairly clear to see that philosophers such as Derrida changed the way academics analyse literature') made the material easily accessible. Well-placed supporting textual evidence ('Postmodernists suggest that truth is no longer verifiable and that new art forms are best created by freely mixing previous styles and themes') and visual evidence (the iPod and its publicity material projected on Powerpoint) helped carry conviction.

Presentation two

The first of two presentations on architectural design was very different. While the frequently used 'I' as in, 'I have selected a domestic building, which is Charles Jencks's house…located in Holland Park, London.' maintained a personal tone, the choice of 'domestic building' rather than 'house' and 'located' rather than just 'in Holland Park' ensured a close association with the Latinate language of academia. This remained consistently so. 'The Jencks house conversion is an example of Postmodern architecture that has been sympathetically related to its context, retaining some of the local features and vernacular style of the London stock brick, cream stucco and trim. The complex hybridism of the façade communicates symbolism, new classicism and mannerism. It has been termed symbolic by its owner, meaning to allow the viewer to appreciate its expressive form and discover its intended message.'

111

The Jencks house, side elevation (after alterations)
Charles Jencks and Terry Farrell, 1978–81

'The conversion of the Jencks' family home, which was built in 1840, evolved over the years 1978–1981. The main conversion shell was designed in collaboration with Terry Farrell Architectural Partnership, and Charles and Maggie Keswick Jencks, the owners.'

112

The Jencks house, front door
Charles Jencks and Terry Farrell, 1978–81

'The treatment of the front entrance door was a deliberate attempt to reconcile function (the door's ironmongery) with the body image.'

Presentation three

A comparable list of Postmodern characteristics, 'irony, pastiche, intertextuality, reflexivity and multiple meanings,' provided a point of reference in a presentation on the cartoon-TV series, *The Simpsons*. All of these were supported with evidence from both theoretical statements and commentaries and illustrated with examples from the series. But they were already announced in the introductory conjunction: 'Postmodernism can be defined as a procedural rebellion against totalizing systems of thought with an eventual affirmation of no centers of value' (Luca Petryshyn, Concordia University) was set against quotes from *The Simpsons*: 'It's po-mo (blank stares all round) Post-modern! (more staring) Yeah, all right – weird for the sake of weird.' (Moe on a work of art in his renovated bar). The ironical humour of the cartoons was echoed in the presentation.

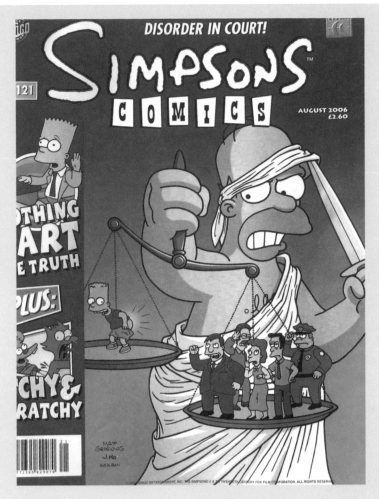

113

Simpsons comic, August 2006

'It's po-mo (blank stares all round) Post-modern! (more staring) Yeah, all right – weird for the sake of weird.' (Moe on a work of art in his renovated bar).

Presentation four

The second presentation on architectural design remained impersonal throughout. The nearest to the personalised 'I' being, 'we can say that'. But while terms such as 'signification', 'appropriation' and 'deconstruction', or sentences such as 'Frank Gehry...juxtaposes various sources...revealing the meaning in the non-narrative manner of detached signifiers', brought the presentation close to a spoken academic essay, the following sentence: 'The effect of the towers composed in a fluid embrace is still extraordinarily lyrical, a show-stopping performance.' is nearer to the more accessible and suggestive language of journalism.

114

Nationale-Nederlanden building, Prague
Frank O. Gehry with Vladimir Milunic 1992–96

'The building...was to fill an empty space in the centre of Prague after World War II bombing'.

WOW, WOW, WOW, WOW, WOW, WOW, WOW, WOW, WOW... WOW, WOW WOW wo

115

Wow wow
Sara Colding, 2005

The use of the body as the sole medium of communication and the spoken, written or printed word reduced to phonetics, as in this piece of graphic illustration, are frequent features of contemporary theatre, fine art and design. But however much they remind us of the possible options available to someone giving an oral presentation, they should also be viewed as cautionary examples. If you wish to communicate as clearly as possible, the audience, the context, appropriate language and mode of delivery must be seriously considered.

Choosing the appropriate language

It is generally assumed that the informal language we use in everyday conversation is the most spontaneous. Made up on the spot with little or no conscious selection, it is easily taken to be natural. But how spontaneous is it? The words and sentences do not select themselves. Much of what we say is a matter of habit: patterns of speech acquired from the wider culture that we repeat over and over again. These are most often common patterns of speech used by all in the group: the well-worn clichés that facilitate easy understanding.

These common patterns of speech are, therefore, a valuable element in all verbal communication but they are restrictive, limiting what can be said. Where the context requires going beyond the mundane, other kinds of language must be used. The discourse surrounding any specialist discipline requires an appropriate specialist vocabulary and this is much the same whether the language is oral or written. Deciding what kind or kinds of language to use in any given context involves some consideration of several important factors. But the considerations do not end with the choice of language. Most oral presentations are delivered live in front of an audience. The presentation is a performance in which the voice and the body contribute to the overall effect.

The audience

The first key question in choosing the appropriate language is who is being addressed. In a one-to-one conversation with a fellow student from the same social and cultural background a great number of assumptions about language communication can be made by both but this could be disastrous in a comparable conversation with a fellow student from a very different cultural and linguistic context, even one within the same peer group. In the absence of a universal language, translation from one particular language into another is hazardous.

Even within the same language culture sharp differences in the use and understanding of words and concepts exist between one social group and another. As we have already seen, subcultural or specialist language can contribute to effective communication between members of the same group or confuse and even alienate those outside it. Whether a listener or reader understands terms like iconography, signifier, *sachlichkeit* or tag, depends upon the breadth and depth of their cultural awareness.

The context

A second key question is what is the context. In the most informal studio situation almost anything that manages to communicate effectively is acceptable, including near-meaningful repetitions such as: 'basically' or 'like', phrases or sentences that trail off into, 'and so on', or slang words as in, 'Dalí's work is whacky'.

This kind of language is unlikely to suit a group discussion involving a more diverse group of participants and be even less appropriate in the context of a student giving an account of their own work to a peer group of international students. Colloquialisms such as, 'higgledy-piggledy' may be acceptable if not encouraged; slang is not. In a pre-prepared oral presentation, standard English and standard diction (or the received equivalents in any other language) are generally expected. This does not exclude elisions, similes, metaphors or the personlised 'I', but it does entail respect for a more formal, public-minded approach in which academic and technical terms are used accurately and theoretical statements are made in the vocabulary particular to each one. It also entails respect for differences in culture, race, gender, and sexual orientation. Prioritising white, heterosexual, male Westerners over all others is no longer acceptable.

116

Circular text
Sara Colding, 2005

The presentation of words here is very different from the same student's previous illustration (page 136). Parallels can be made with how important it is to give serious consideration to the elements in an oral presentation. Legibility in print is like clear vocal delivery: the context well judged and the subject made accessible to the audience.

Delivery

At whatever level, from the most informal conversation to the most formal oral presentation, spoken delivery is never exclusively dependent upon the language used. Vocal characteristics, the way the voice inflects and gives emphasis to words and phrases, is an important contributory factor in communicating meaning. But verbal, vocal and visual communication overlap. Facial and body performance can decisively influence the reception and understanding of what is being said. Consider the case of identical twins in an interview, both making exactly the same statements in exactly the same tone of voice, accent and emphases, but one facially and bodily rigid, the other physically animated and expressive. The effect of each would be very different and give rise to different interpretations. Just as there is no universal language, there is no universal performance and no universal interpretation.

Dividing, headlines
Louise Matell, 2005

Assessing the context, carefully judging the target audience, choosing the right language, verbal or visual, and deciding on the most effective mode of delivery, are not restricted to oral presentations. This image shows attempts by a graphic design student to identify different kinds of language used in different English newspapers to report the same event.

Nationale-Nederlanden building, Prague
Frank O Gehry with
Vladimir Milunic 1992–96

In her oral presentation on Gehry's building, the student stressed the Postmodern concern to go beyond any single, elitist interpretation of a building to include more readily accessible elements, especially visual metaphors. The two contrasted but embracing towers are a visual metaphor for a dancing couple: the Ginger and Fred of popular Hollywood culture. In this way architects aim to communicate meaning to an ordinary person while keeping the interest of experts. Might this be a consideration for those giving an oral presentation?

Sampling one

A sample identifies an object, action or conduct judged worthy of imitation; an illustration of a typical or representative example. A sample can serve as a model for others. In many ways, not least our choice of language, we are all dependent on existing models, whether we imitate a single one, reject one in favour of another, or combine elements from several. Within visual culture, the term eclectic is used where the artist/designer has taken elements from several sources and synthesised these into their own creative work. A related term, intertextuality, recognises that all verbal and visual constructs depend upon other, already existing texts for their meaning.

To sample an existing model is to evaluate its qualities; to test its worth or suitability. When we are impressed by a particularly effective oral or written presentation, we almost inevitably file it away for future reference or use. It becomes a measure, a way of evaluating what is appropriate or inappropriate, successful or unsuccessful. While reading through the preceding, albeit very edited, statements by students, we have probably critically assessed their suitability and effectiveness in each context.

Here we recall the most common ways in which we verbalise the visual; it is generally these criteria we use to help us decide what is worth imitating, or at least learning from.

Naming

Every example of studio talk used in this chapter names people, things, thoughts, actions, events and much else. Naming is a fundamental in all language communication. In the context of verbalising the visual, nouns (the words we use to name things) and adjectives (the words used to qualify a noun) play a vital role in any commentary: they identify things. Our understanding of anything spoken or written depends upon the speaker or writer naming the subject and everything else relating to that subject. But there is rarely only one name for something and even more adjectives to qualify it. When you read through the preceding student statements or listen to anyone talking about something visual, ask yourself not only how important are the names used but how appropriate are the chosen names. Are any of these samples worthy of imitation? Are they instructive?

Describing

Naming is rarely enough to adequately identify a visual experience; the context is almost always too complex for that. Simply naming the objects and actions in a major painting would not only be inadequate, it would very likely be misleading. Further information explaining the relationship between the objects and actions and how these are represented is required. If our first experience of a visual image is through someone's verbal description, the subsequent sight of the actual image poses a direct test of just how effectively words were used to recreate its manifest appearance. Does the verbal experience match the visual one? There are lessons to be learned from such comparisons and these are increased where there are several verbal descriptions of the same visual image. Which one serves as the best model for your needs?

Contextualising

Neither the visual image nor anything said or written about it exists in a cultural vacuum. Both are directly linked to a set of assumptions, expectations and outcomes. This is as true of professional products of art and design and the discourse that surrounds them as it is of student work and the related discussion. The distinction between the two is the context. Professional designers work to real briefs with contractual obligations. Most student design assignments are closer to exercises, stages towards the acquisition of professional status. To achieve any proper appreciation of a student's work, it is necessary first of all to know what the conditions of the brief are. Students in the same group who already know this can quickly move on to giving a context for their interpretation and final realisation of the assignment, as the students quoted in this chapter do. But there is no single correct way of doing this. When we assess the alternatives for our own purposes we must keep in mind what is or is not appropriate.

Analysing

Analysing the subject or artefact being discussed is similarly enlightening but it is generally more difficult. It requires an ability to deconstruct the artefact into its constituent elements whether these are its structural components, the formal vocabulary employed, the ideological motivations that inform it, or all of these. Inevitably, this also involves familiarity with a number of ideological positions and the specialist vocabulary associated with these. Several of the preceding student examples address these complex matters but how well do you think they do it? Can any one of these serve as a model of good practice? If not, might elements from each be combined to do so? Whatever the conclusion, it is well to remember that there is sometimes as much to be learned from a failed performance as a successful one.

Interpreting

Interpretations of the same artefact can vary immensely as can the language used to do this. Once we accept that verbal and visual representations are ambiguous, it is inevitable that there will be many equally valid readings of the same thing. When we add to this an awareness of how much the meaning we attribute to objects is determined by our personal experiences and knowledge, the range of possible interpretations becomes even wider as does the variety of language used. Only in the case of a particular ideological interpretation, as in a Marxist or psychoanalytical reading, is the language very specific. In almost all other interpretations, it is hybrid, drawing on as many existing models as are required by the speaker. This, perhaps, is the model to adopt when we are faced with the difficulty of interpreting a complex work. We too must accept eclecticism, mixing and matching the language according to need.

Evaluating

In the context of discussing visual culture just as much as in any other discussion, we repeatedly make value judgements. Our evaluation may be made without any supporting evidence or even explanation but it still expresses an assessment of worth. How often do we begin sentences with, 'I like…' or, 'I don't like…'? On a personal, subjective level this is acceptable but where more objective criteria are required, it is not. Student assignments include the criteria for assessment; it is the obligation of the student to meet as many of these as possible. Measuring their success is the central activity of any evaluation. But what kind of language is used to do this? Is the vocabulary used adequate to the task? Is it capable of making subtle distinctions of worth? Do the judgements made consistently refer back to the stated criteria? Deciding which assessments fulfil this last requirement is relatively easy. Deciding which of these employs language in the most effective way is less so.

Summary

1

Spoken language is generally informal and colloquial.

2

Tone of voice, accent, emphasis, all influence understanding.

3

Clear enunciation and pronunciation using standard diction are essential when addressing a diverse audience.

4

The listener, unlike the reader, has only a single occasion in which to hear and understand.

7

In interviews, the interviewer is usually in control.

10

Remember that facial and body language influence interpretation and understanding.

5

Inconclusive, faltering delivery is acceptable in spontaneous speech.

8

Pre-prepared oral presentations presuppose more formal language and a clear structure.

6

Oral accounts often invite a narrative structure, a chronological sequencing of elements.

9

Choose the right language to suit your audience and the context.

05 The essay

05

The essay

119

Stencil graffiti
anonymous, 2006

Graffiti in all or any of its forms is of considerable interest to very many students of visual culture, influencing their own creative work, frequently the topic of conversation and a subject to be written about. The specific vocabulary used to discuss graffiti is common to all of these contexts but the colloquial language of ordinary speech is not appropriate in a formal essay which must fulfil other expectations.

Expectations

For students of visual culture, the formal academic essay is the most common context in which they are expected to write about their specialist subject. Writing an essay is the occasion when expectations require the kinds of specialist written language associated with the professional world of academic art and design history, theory and criticism. The informal colloquialisms, elisions, fragmented sentences and phrases of oral communication are not appropriate in a formal essay, as one student acknowledged: 'Banksy's anonymity is – excuse the colloquialism – a very cool aspect of his work'.

The essay form

The origin of the English word 'essay' is French. The French verb 'essayer' means to try, to attempt or to make a trial of something, hence the still extant meaning of an essayist, someone who carries out a test or trial; an essai. This is very close to the modern English meaning. To write a 'paper', in the sense of a written answer to a question, is an alternative word although this can also identify an oral presentation made at a conference.

If an essay is the most academic piece of writing students are asked to produce, it is clearly an advantage to be as well informed as possible about the history, theory and criticism of visual culture as well as the specialist language used in these disciplines. But what, in general, is expected of an essay?

There is no single way of writing an essay. But, whatever the given title or question, the essay should be: clearly structured, the structure reinforcing the development of a particular point of view or argument; written in standard English (or its appropriate equivalent); and comply with the university's or college's agreed practice of academic presentation. The last demand can vary considerably. There are several internationally acceptable ways of identifying sources, references and quotations.

Given the open-ended, inconclusive character of an essay it is not surprising that most examples engage in a variety of equally relevant activities, the most common being those of describing, contextualising, analysing, interpreting and evaluating. It is equally likely to be the case that the language will not only employ the specific vocabulary and terminology relevant to any particular ideological position but a range of linguistic devices from the most matter of fact and denotative to the sometimes highly connotative, in which similes and metaphors play an important role. The kinds of language required to address the visible, material elements of an object, locate it in a particular cultural milieu and explain what it might signify are different.

The essay structure

A majority of good essays have a basic three-part structure, the activating force being the development of a well-supported, convincing argument. Just as the sequence of events in a well-constructed narrative or account most often depend upon there being a clear beginning, middle and end to the story, so do very many good essays. In an essay, this structure breaks down into defining the subject, exploring the subject and drawing conclusions. Really good essays, of course, are more complex than this generalised framework suggests but overall they often follow this pattern.

Given the importance of pursuing an argument or point of view, it follows that the main substance in an academic essay is within the middle section. It is here that both the breadth and depth of any student's knowledge and awareness will reveal itself. It is also the context in which a student's familiarity with and ability to use often-difficult concepts and vocabulary will be called upon.

There are occasions when an assignment may ask for an account or brief history of a subject but these are rare and more likely to be only a part of a much wider requirement. With extended essays and final year dissertations where the word count runs into several thousand and not several hundred, the need for a historical perspective requires more detailed information.

Stencil graffiti
Banksy, 2005

'Like a curator for the whole city (Banksy) decides where his images would "hang" best.'

Generally rich in similes and metaphors, this single statement from the first student's essay implicitly sees the urban environment as the equivalent of a gallery with Banksy's work as a major exhibitor. But it also interprets and evaluates Banksy's work.

Suited to both the essay form and the particular requirements of the given assignment, all the essays quoted in this chapter address their subject in an interrogative way, trying to discover possible answers rather than claiming to know them in advance. The essay assignment titled Explorative Study asked students to examine possible sources of influence on their own work.

The first two essays quoted here (figs. 120 and 121) focussed on the work of stencil graffitist Banksy. The introduction to one essay echoes the title, 'I want to explore his work in much more depth,' while the other one implicitly accepts the need for close investigation by stating, 'His work lives among us and for the most part goes unnoticed.'

Going underground,
carriage interior
Ken Kirton, 2005

'It is Banksy's philosophy which connects my work to date with his. For my 'Going Underground' project I put up posters on an underground train in order to give the public an unexpected interpretation of the person sitting across from them and to amuse them.'

This matter-of-fact statement by the second student directly addresses the central task of the assignment. But in following Banksy's aim to provoke a public response, the student has used the space allocated to commercial advertisements in an underground train carriage instead of a wall.

Corporate US flag
Adbusters, 2002

This third essay was written in response to an assignment, the key task of which was: 'to write… a critical survey of contemporary theory and practice in a chosen specialist area', in this case magazine design.

Like the other two essays, this used a three-part structure. The argument focused on the differences between commercial magazines dependent upon 'funding from advertisements', and with a 'seamless flow between magazine articles and advertisements', and Adbusters, 'the anti-corporate advertising magazine'.

123

**Going underground,
Leaving the platform
Fernando Ribeiro Rodrigues Junior,
2005**

In both his creative work and the
written essay this student's
commitment to graffiti and graffiti-
inspired art and design is very
evident but his careful examination
of the essay brief ensured his text
went beyond the usual excited
enthusiasm to a close analysis and
evaluation of the subject that
resulted in a well-supported point
of view.

Interpreting the assignment

It is sometimes claimed that there are fundamentally only a handful of essay titles or questions, and it is true that even a cursory glance at the questions set on any undergraduate programme reveals how frequently some words occur in stating the demands of the assignment. Analyse, compare, contrast, criticise, define, describe and evaluate, together with examine, explain and illustrate, very nearly complete the list. But none of these words is exclusive of the others. To analyse something involves critical examination. To define something involves describing and explaining. To explain something involves interpretation and evaluation.

The two essays quoted here are revealing in unexpected ways. Each presents a different response to the Explorative Study brief yet both include original work produced for a studio design assignment, Going Underground. Both respond directly to the explicit tasks but reveal awareness of the implicit expectations. The first goes directly into the source of influence, an introductory paragraph stating:

'epistemology (questioning the bases of knowledge) is one of the greatest influences on my work'.

The other, following the now standard model of good practice, provides an introductory statement, 'I will carry out an in-depth enquiry...I will also aim to discover any motivating ideas or stimulating theories...pointing out any similarities that evidently stem from ideas that have been inspired by other artists,' and vigorously pursuing these through to a confirmatory conclusion.

124

Going underground,
The Darkness
Fernando Ribeiro Rodrigues Junior,
2005

'It seems like there is a great trend in contemporary art of using child-like-badly-drawn-refined-dada-collages as a medium for expression.'

Although fulfilling almost all the explicit and implicit requirements of the Explorative Study brief, this quotation from an otherwise articulate student's essay reveals just how difficult it can be to verbalise the visual. The string of hyphenated adjectives betrays concern in finding the right words to describe the particular 'trend'.

125

Going Underground,
Don't All Be So Sad
Martin Richardson, 2005

This student's interpretation of the brief went beyond 'a movement, group or individual' source of influence, 'things that inspire me...are my everyday experiences in the environment in which I live', but became more specific in terms of the Going Underground design assignment:

'I now notice that every journey I make is completely different to the previous and I do not know what to expect of my next expedition.'

This explorative, open-ended approach was well suited to the stated tasks.

Assessing the Brief

Essay titles or questions are usually short if not always precise. A tutor who asks students to explain something is unlikely to include in the brief that they also interpret and evaluate. The student, however, would be wise to assume that both are expected. Most texts contain a subtext. Interrogating the text of an essay brief, identifying the implicit as well as explicit demands, can lead to a deeper understanding of what is expected. Using the binary system of opposites to question the brief can also add to understanding: identifying what is not said illuminates what is said.

Consider this essay title: 'Compare and contrast the theory and practice of William Morris and Christopher Dresser.' Some students would know that Morris was a key figure in the English Arts and Crafts Movement while his contemporary, Dresser, was a key figure in the movement to reform 19th century industrial design, but the brief makes no mention of this. The alert student would also realise that the brief implicitly expects them to address what is similar and dissimilar between the two designer-theorists.

Some essay briefs are less prescriptive; more concerned with defining the parameters, the overall limits of any possible response, than determining outcomes. Consider for example this 'Explorative Study' brief:

'Choose a movement, group or individual artist or designer that you can identify as a source of stimulation, inspiration or encouragement. Carry out an in-depth enquiry into your chosen subject, examining the social and historical context, the motivating ideas or theories and the distinguishing characteristics of the work. Then show in what way you have been influenced by the individual group or movement.'

The title is instructive, pre-empting any demand for a conclusive response. The most explicit requirements are 'identify', 'enquire', 'examine' and 'show', but, as before, unstated expectations such as the need to describe, analyse and evaluate are implicit.

If in assessing the brief any student fails to identify and acknowledge the unstated, implicit requirements, it is most likely that they will not achieve as full a response in their essay as they might. It is we who interpret verbal statements and we must take responsibility for our interpretations. Of course, the brief may be unclear. Where this is a possibility, consult the tutor/lecturer who set it and ask for clarification. It is advantageous to have every possible expectation of the brief identified.

Researching the brief

Whatever the demands and expectations, the writing of a formal academic essay requires some research. For undergraduate students, it is very likely that the set brief is one directly related to a current or recent programme of study that includes lectures, seminars and possibly tutorials. If the lecturer has given a good presentation, students will have experienced an introduction in which the key issues and even key words were identified; an introduction that greatly assists in deciding what is important, less important and of little importance in what follows. Seminar discussions offer the opportunity to question and clarify these issues. A tutorial can address any particular concerns of the individual student.

Having decided the requirements of the essay brief, specific areas of research can be identified. Using key words and concepts, these can be pursued in library catalogues, the Internet and elsewhere to source appropriate material. Contemporary media offer not only a wide range of sources but different kinds and levels of information on a single subject. If the subject being researched is unfamiliar, then specialist dictionaries, encyclopedias and books introducing the relevant subject can provide a generalised overview and possibly some useful reference material for further research, as can websites. Ensure that the material is up to date or, at least, still relevant and that it is of a suitably academic kind.

For a majority of undergraduates engaged in the practice of one or another medium within visual culture, the academic components of their programme of study are most likely to focus on the key words, issues and periods of Modernism and Postmodernism. This no more means an acceptance of these terms than it does their suitability for other than Western or Westernised cultures. Try pursuing words such as, imperialism, post-colonialism or identity and the varieties and complexities of response will become increasingly evident. All research is determined by the researcher or on the advice of their tutor. Just as each essay offers a particular point of view, so the research that informs it was motivated by a particular set of interests. These interests might evolve or change through the research but they are always decided by the individual.

Recording information

The language employed in any research context can vary considerably and recording it can be problematic. The use of key words and concepts should be respected but bearing these exceptions in mind, the general advice is to use your own words when making notes in a lecture or seminar, from books, websites, or from anywhere else. This will help ensure your understanding of the material as well as steering you away from unintended plagiarism. Editing your notes on the same day they were made can clarify their meaning while the original experience is still fresh.

No one who has experienced listening to a speaker, looking at the visual images and trying to make a useful record of both would deny that it is difficult. But practising students of the visual arts are more likely to be able to communicate verbally and visually than other students. Given that the recorded material is for the student's own use, brevity and even personal coding can be used. The priority is that the information should be easily retrievable at a later date as required.

Another student's response to the 'Explorative Study' brief took the research back into his secondary school experiences. These earlier influences, especially that of photography, were linked to current ones through statements such as, 'The images that have always stayed in my mind are the posters from the Russian Bolshevik era,' adding later that an 'interest in symbolism and power has always been at the back of my mind'.

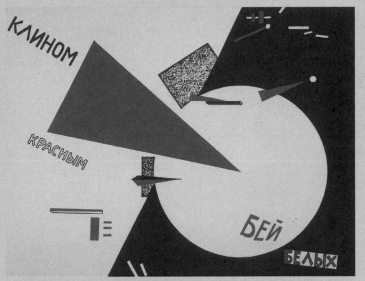

Beat the Whites with the Red Wedge
El Lissitsky, 1919

Exploring influences during his teenage years this student later recognised, 'as I became more politically aware I looked into political imagery…. Political posters have always been used to direct and manipulate people…they opened my mind to what type of imagery I could achieve.' Lissitsky's poster supporting the Soviet revolution is an iconic example of how composition and proportion reduced to their most abstract elements can realise a powerful image.

Untitled photograph
Joseph Owen, 2005

'This photograph gives an example of a personal attempt of trying to capture an image in the style of Bresson.' Bresson's decisive moment is when the camera records an image in which form and content are matched and in researching material for this essay this student discovered Bresson's later involvement in and influence on the Magnum group of photographers.

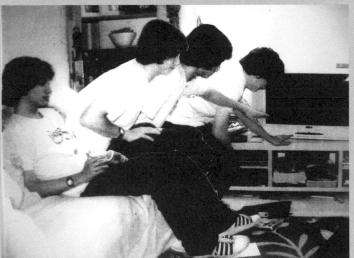

Untitled photograph
Joseph Owen, 2005

Further exploration led to other beneficial discoveries:

'I came across a photographer who would stretch my imagination even further. Duane Michals would not just capture images on his camera, but he would manipulate them and create bizarre sequences and scenarios…. Using him as an influence led me to create my own sequence.'

Recording all this information in the context of the essay tests the verbal skills of any student.

129

**Rear view of a woman
before a mirror
Heylen Espinosa-Casallas, 2006**

An exploration of her reactions to
representations of women, this
student's essay had a very decided
point of view ('Women may not stay
at home any longer but we now see
them everywhere, used to advertise
an eclectic range of products from
cars to underwear'). This was most
clearly stated in its analysis and
critical evaluation of the
photographer, Helmut Newton. Her
own photographic work, including
this image, is a riposte to his.
('Unlike Newton, I chose not to
capture myself in this shot.')

Writing the essay

There is no shortage of books offering advice on how to write an essay and in recent years an increasing number of these have specifically addressed writing about the visual arts. All offer some kind of sequential model to follow, from initial reception of the brief through research to writing and presenting the finished piece. In practice, all prove to be in their differing ways idealistic. Some students only make a clear assessment of what the brief requires after they have begun researching the subject. The material discovered during research can easily influence how to interpret the brief, decide the point of view and ultimately the argument. But once the point of view is decided, it inevitably suggests what kind of research is required and what sort of supporting evidence is needed. This toing and froing is a common experience and involves examination, interpretation and evaluation at every stage in the process.

**The Eiffel Tower,
Georges Pierre Seurat, 1889**

For the first student, 'Modernist artists such as Seurat admired the Tower immensely', so much so that he painted his first image 'before the construction was completed.' The student then noted that 'Seurat and Eiffel also shared key interests' in matters of design and their common desire to rationalise their methods. Seurat's decision to paint the Tower before it's completion is especially unusual in the context of the nearly unanimous negative reaction to it and is a clear indicator of his modernist sympathies.

**The Eiffel Tower, Paris,
Gustave Eiffel, 1889**

For the second student, 'it is not only modern materials that caused the tower to be constructed in iron, but also modernist design principles: form follows function.' This reference to Louis Sullivan's quintessentially Modernist claim that 'form ever follows function' both contextualises Eiffel's Tower and underpins its own Modernist credentials.

In their response to the demanding essay question 'What is Modernism?', with its instruction to choose two artefacts to 'argue why each is modern rather than just a product of its time', two students overlapped in choosing Gustave Eiffel's Tower. Both recognised that innovative representations of modern urbanised culture, like the Degas image reproduced here, had already been achieved by the 1880s, but that Eiffel's Tower became a symbol of this modernity. Their interpretations, however, differed. Where one focused on the rationalist argument within Modernism ('I will explore the rationalist links' between the tower and George Seurat's Bathers at Asniéres), the other focused on the urbanisation of culture ('In the second half of the Industrial Revolution large cities became a focal point for not only business and government but also for creativity'), closely relating the Tower to the Seurat and later Robert Delaunay series of images of the Tower. Both students drew upon a substantial range of supporting material: the first adopting a loosely dialectical model; the second comparing differing responses.

**Bathers at Asniéres
Georges Pierre Seurat, 1884**

'It is believed that his rationalised methods meant that he was always in control of what he was producing.' Seurat's rationalised methods included the use of mathematical systems of proportion and composition and a systematic use of the divided colour dabs used by the Impressionists to re-create the sparkle of natural sunlight.

**Place de la Concorde
Edgar Degas c.1876**

'The big influential urban environments of the civilised world became cultural capitals,' and the redevelopment of Paris after 1853 epitomised this. But it is not only Degas's choice of an urban subject that makes his image modern, it is the cropped, fragmented way in which the subject is represented. The Impressionist group, in which Degas was a central figure, is considered to be the first Modernist movement.

Selecting the appropriate material

Just as interrogating the assignment brief can help clarify its requirements, so can interrogating the research material help select what is appropriate to the chosen point of view. But, because the essay requires an argument, the selection of material cannot only be that which supports the chosen point of view. Comparing and contrasting positions, weighing the evidence for and against, are central to the development of a convincing argument and its presentation.

Deciding on a point of view is, therefore, crucial in the writing of an essay. It not only helps select the supporting textual and visual evidence for the point of view, it helps select the equally important contrary evidence. In a well-argued essay, there should be a representative selection of contrary positions, each represented through the appropriate vocabulary and concepts. Exploring the similarities and dissimilarities of language used by these can add considerably to the argument. It can also help clarify the point of view proposed in the essay, identifying the theoretical and ideological sources that contributed to it. If there is recognition of these sources of influence before the essay is written, it is very likely that the essay will be greatly improved.

But the sources used must be reliable. This can be a complicated issue. There is no certain way of knowing which is the more reliable between texts supported with primary research evidence or those supported with secondary research evidence. (Primary research is that carried out at first hand. Secondary research is the use of material discovered by others.) If the use of primary research without convincing, supporting evidence is questionable, the use of secondary source material is equally so. However persuasive a commentary on whatever subject, we may not need to know if it is by an expert but we do need to know if it is valid on its own or supported with accurately reported or quoted evidence. This too can be problematic. Where the main text of a book quotes another but does not identify the source, the quotation cannot be used with any reliability in an essay unless the original source can be found. Asking all these questions can help clarify matters. In general, it is the status of the author (it is well to research this) and the reputation of the publisher that helps decide.

Evaluating the research material

There are key questions to ask about the available material. Does the material rely upon primary, secondary or both types of research? The first offers new evidence and probably a new point of view but is relatively untested. The second can be reassuring if only because it quotes sources already familiar from lectures, seminars and general reading. The third is possibly revisionist, questioning the various received interpretations and proposing possible alternatives in the light of new evidence.

It follows that reading several accounts and interpretations of the subject is beneficial. Ask yourself what convincing evidence is given? Does the text rely upon the exposition of a logical argument or the use of unreliable similes, ambiguous metaphors and a whole range of rhetorical literary devices? All of which, as we have seen, are common in writing about the visual arts and can very easily persuade the reader to accept any number of assumptions and unproven, prejudiced positions. No text ever brings its own guarantee of authority. It is for the reader to interpret and decide, as it is for the reader of any written essay.

This is a crucial factor. If we, as reader, have to decide what is or is not reliable material, on what basis can we decide? In such circumstances, beware the temptation to conclude that only experts know. Consider the questions raised in the above two paragraphs. Use these questions to interrogate the research material. If the overall balance is positive, it is likely that the material is both useful and reliable. Should this prove so, then ask yourself, how does this relate or support my point of view? How can I use this material in an effective way?

Structuring an argument

Once you have decided upon a point of view, you are able to propose your position for consideration. This is the first stage in the development of your argument. In academic terms, it is your thesis and you will want to reinforce your position with the most convincing, supporting evidence that you can. Make sure that you present your point of view as clearly as possible using the appropriate language. As with most declarations of intent, it is as important to state what you will not be addressing as what you will. This helps define the parameters of your essay. The title and subtitle of your essay should indicate its central concerns.

Your research, however, will have drawn your attention to differing and even contrary opinions to your own. These alternatives need to be examined if you are to properly consider the evidence for and against. They are the antithesis of your own position and form the second stage in the development of your argument. These contrary points of view need as much attention and supporting evidence, verbal and visual, as that required by the main thesis. They also require paying attention to the sometimes quite different, specialist vocabulary. Remember how a consideration of binary opposites can reveal the position of an author. It is not unusual for a superficially persuasive, if ultimately unconvincing, point of view to rely upon a rhetorical use of language. Make sure that the evidence you use in support of your own point of view employs convincing language, convincingly used.

The third stage involves making a critical evaluation of all this material, weighing one position against another in order to arrive at whatever conclusion you can. It is here that the possibility arises of resolving the conflict between thesis and antithesis to make a synthesis. Thesis, antithesis and synthesis are the three stages in the process of dialectical reasoning, the process during which opposing points of view are ultimately reconciled into a higher order. It is this process that underpins almost all the advice offered on how to develop an argument in a formal, academic essay. This three-part structure is attributed to the early 19th century German philosopher, G. W. F. Hegel. But Hegel's model almost invariably assumes a conclusive end to the process of dialectical reasoning. A conclusive end may not be available and this must be recognised. It is perfectly valid to end an otherwise thoroughly investigative essay on a question mark.

Organising the evidence

The thesis, antithesis, synthesis model has been tested and proven valuable in incalculable numbers of essays, dissertations and theses but it is an abstract model. If your assignment brief restricts you to 1250–1500 words, you may have no more than six short paragraphs in which to deal with all three stages of the process. The greater the number of words, the greater the number of paragraphs. After 2000 words the paragraphs can be fitted into subsections.

Quantity and quality should not be equated but it is easy to see that as the number of permitted words increases so does the need to find the most appropriate subsection and paragraph in which they might best serve the development of the argument. Parallels have been suggested between the structure of a good narrative with its beginning, middle and end, and that of an essay. However, in the sequencing of the stages in an argument, it is the dramatist not the novelist who provides a more suitable model. An argument is more like the dialogue between different speakers than a story told by a single person from their point of view.

How best, therefore, to stage the argument? What approach might be thought the most suitable? Yet again, there is no single answer to these questions but a serious consideration of some of the most widely practised options can help resolve the difficulty. The deciding factor, however, might very well be the temperament of the essayist: an awareness of what best suits the writer can quickly eliminate any number of unsuitable options.

Consider the following two possibilities in response to the same material. In the first option, contrary points of view to that of the essayist are directly challenged, their understood limitations exposed. In the second option, the essayist endorses any elements in the alternative points of view that are in sympathy with their own but rejects the others. The first option effectively clears the field for the essayist's own point of view. The second adopts a revisionist approach, modifying existing points of view to arrive at a new one.

Both the above models engage with and evaluate differing points of view. They generate dialogue in order to arrive at either an alternative position or a synthesis of existing ones. A much more rare third approach is to examine and evaluate all or at least a representative range of differing points of view but in revealing the inherent limitations of all of these to conclude that there is no available certainty: all points of view are relative.

A limitation on the number of words is not necessarily a limitation in arguing a point of view. Another student's response to the 'Explorative Study' brief hinged upon the centrally placed statement, 'Although I really like the aesthetic qualities of Helmut Newton's work…. I cannot help but…despise the way he represented women,' both positions being explored.

Nor did a similar limitation on words hinder the development of a well-supported argument in another student's response to the brief, 'What is Modernism?' Fritz Lang's 1927 film Metropolis and Sant'Elia's 1914 Citta Nuova project were cited in the argument. 'Both these texts are focused on the idea of the city…epicentres of culture, technology and advancement…. Both artists…used New York as a starting point for their work.'

134

Untitled photograph
Heylen Espinosa-Casallas, 2005

Helmut Newton's Vivian F., Hotel
Volney, New York, 1972 has a semi-
naked woman sitting cross-legged,
head on a raised hand, looking out
of the picture. 'The fact that it has
been set in a hotel bedroom,
portrays a certain level of coldness,
objectivity and impersonal
relationship between the
photographer and the model. In
response to Newton's photograph I
have...set mine somewhere
familiar...the big windows behind
me represents my freedom and
where I want to be. The street
represents where society wants me
to be and the fact that my face is not
in the frame is saying "I don't want
to be part of this." Vivian F.'s cleavage
is rather visible, whereas any
possible chances of mine being seen
have been overruled by the position
of my arm.' The student's statement
is interpretation and critical
analysis of both photographs.

135

Metropolis
Fritz Lang, 1927

The argument that the condition of
modernity is essentially that of an
urban-industrial culture is well
supported in this student's essay.
'This was a time of huge change
and advancement socially.... The
Industrial Revolution had
transformed life, the world had
entered the mechanised age. Huge
factories were producing the
machines of the modern age, this
led to an enormous shift in lifestyle
for everyone but particularly those
living in cities.' Working in the
relatively new medium of film,
itself a mechanical form of
representation, Lang's *Metropolis*
is one of the earliest examples
of a cinematic response to the
burgeoning urban-industrial
culture.

136

La Cittá Nuova
Antonio Sant'Elia, 1913

'Modernist work should not dwell
on its time or just be comfortable, it
should be looking ahead.... It must
embrace modern ideas and
concepts and be able to represent
these in a new way...it must
innovate and improve on the
products of its time', argues the
student, and appropriately so. An
Italian Futurist architect and
decisively avant-garde, Sant'Elia
responded to the rapid urban-
industrial changes surrounding
him. '[His] New City is a series of
drawings and paintings that detail
his plans for a modern city for his
generation...a new city of glass,
steel and concrete.'

Presenting the essay

The subsections and paragraphs of the argument are certainly the most substantial part of the essay, but the overall structure is greater than this. There is still the need for an introduction and conclusion. A proper conclusion can only be written after the argument is complete. Some have suggested that the introduction too should be left until later. The reasoning is that it is possibly reckless to state what you will do until you are sure you have done it.

Either way, an introduction raises certain expectations. It should clearly state the subject and identify the important issues raised by the assignment brief. It should set the parameters of the essay, declaring what will and will not be addressed. An explanation of how the essay will do these things completes the introduction.

The conclusion, like the introduction, the argument and the complete essay, is another three-part structure. In this case, it should summarise the key points of the essay, the central argument, and whatever conclusions have been drawn. The conclusion need not be conclusive but it should bring the threads of the essay towards a satisfactory end.

A crucial factor here is pacing; the overall rhythm and momentum of the unfolding text. Some of the most successful essays generate the feeling of setting out with a clear purpose and successfully leading the reader towards an equally clear conclusion. There is a sense of inevitability to the whole enterprise: a conviction that the argument could only lead towards this particular end. Achieving this high level of persuasive writing requires considerable literary skill. Sample just a handful of books on the history of art and design and it becomes very evident that possessing great knowledge is not synonymous with possessing the verbal skills required to successfully communicate this knowledge. Verbalising the visual is always a challenge.

Using formal academic language

No student at the outset of their undergraduate studies can be expected to have much knowledge of the vast range of vocabulary and concepts used in the specialist language of art and design history and theory or any other related disciplines. It is enough at this early stage that they have some awareness of the linguistic practices – simile, metaphor, describing or analysing, for example – used in academic writing. It is wise, therefore, to proceed with caution.

Never use a word or concept you do not properly understand. Use specialist dictionaries and glossaries to find out what they mean. The same is true for specific theories. Do not adopt a theoretical approach without having a firm grasp of the key ideas, concepts and vocabulary. Whenever a student uses unfamiliar terms it is almost always evident. The terms are not convincingly integrated into the main text. They appear alien to it. First year undergraduates are usually forgiven these awkward intrusions into their texts but they need to be overcome as quickly as possible. They would not be tolerated in a final-year dissertation.

A fourth student's response to the 'What is Modernism?' brief exemplifies the satisfactory relating of introduction, development of the argument, and conclusion. The introductory paragraph acknowledges the need 'to explain the idea of the modern and modernism,' narrowing this to the inter-war 'period in which modernism consolidated its ideas and designs,' and includes the 1925 Dessau Bauhaus building and Mondrian's mature work, as the two chosen artefacts. The final paragraph summarily concludes that: 'Mondrian's work shares its simple stripped down aesthetic with that of…the Bauhaus.' In-between, differences are fully explored.

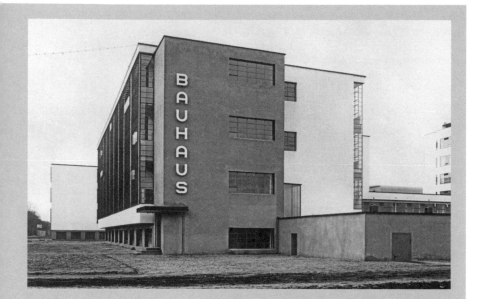

Exterior view of the Bauhaus building, Dessau
Walter Gropius, 1925–26

'The Bauhaus was very much a part of Rationalistic Modernism and was heavily influenced by the machine age and idolisation of technology.' The large glass front, simple, uncomplicated cubed design and use of modern materials such as a concrete structure are all classic characteristics of Modernist architecture.

View from the interior of the Bauhaus building, Dessau
Walter Gropius, 1925–26

In comparing Gropius's Bauhaus with Mondrian's mature paintings the student noted that '[Mondrian's] use of orthogonal (horizontal and vertical) lines were schematic representations'. The grid is the common factor here and clearly visible in this view of the Bauhaus.

The integrated essay

A well-presented essay is one in which all the separate elements are assembled into a coherent whole. Just as the specialist vocabulary and concepts need to be properly integrated into the body of the main text, so do quotations and visual material. It will be obvious if you use a quotation you do not fully understand if only because the terms used in the quotation will probably be at variance with your own in the main text. If the main text does not direct attention to what is relevant in the visual images used, they too will appear detached. Both quotations and visual images should directly contribute to the development of the argument.

This pattern extends to every single element in the essay. Just as the many different threads that are woven into a sample textile must match warp and weft in equal tension if there is to be an even surface texture, so must the diverse elements woven into the text of an essay be equally well integrated. There should be no holes, no gaps in the argument, no lack of supporting textual or visual evidence. The structure should be watertight. When an essay achieves this level of integration of all its elements, it invariably adds greater conviction to the overall argument.

Sampling two

If there is no single way of writing an essay then there can be no single model of good practice. The meaning of the word essay, to make a trial of something, is too inconclusive for that. Nevertheless, there are useful criteria that can help decide whether a particular essay might serve as a model but, as with the most frequently used words in essay questions, these criteria are not exclusive: one criterion implies another. To survey, explore, compare or interrogate involves examining, investigating, questioning, appraising. All the terms overlap with each other. Applying these criteria in a systematic way will give some measure of what is successful and what is less than successful in an essay.

Sampling essays can be a very time-consuming task. Discussing and evaluating the work produced for a practical art or design assignment is frequently done by a group altogether. There is no parallel for this in the assessment of written work. Lifting short quotations from an essay can give only a hint of how these relate to the relevant paragraph let alone the complete text. A summary of the key elements in an essay is an abstraction however much it might indicate the overall scope. So, too, is a breakdown of the stages in the development of an argument. Only the short quotations give any idea of the kind of language used. The only satisfactory way to sample essays is to read them from beginning to end and we do this alone.

Have you ever read through an essay by a fellow student? Have you read several in order to make comparisons? If so, were you judging them by their overall effect or were you looking for specific practices that might help you overcome a problem in your own essay writing? Were you using the essays to improve your writing skills in much the same way that you use the art and design of others to develop your own? These are all useful questions to bear in mind when you read essays or any other texts by someone else.

Interrogate

To fully assess the merits of an essay and decide in what ways it might serve as a model for your own essay writing, it is necessary to ask not only many questions but to do so with rigour. The material must be closely scrutinised and interrogated. If you have already done this to the overall composition and the structure of the argument, you must then do it to the kinds of language used. Few good essays are written in only one kind of language. Is the language too colloquial for an academic essay? Is it closer to journalism than a scholarly text? Or, is the essay text congested with jargon, the unnecessary display of specialist vocabulary and concepts? Does the language assist in clarifying the points made or does it only serve to make them obscure? Getting the balance right is very important. Having learned to interrogate other people's essays you can then do it to your own to ascertain how successful they are.

Compare

Comparing one thing with another helps clarify what is distinctive about something. Similarities and dissimilarities are revealed. If all the possible elements used in an essay are listed, from overall structure to individual words, these can provide a useful basis on which to compare the selected examples. By narrowing down the focus of attention to particular aspects, it can help minimise prejudice and offer a more objective basis for assessing the value of each essay as a model for imitation. At its most mechanical level, this way of assessing the essays can be just a matter of ticks and crosses for each essay against the separate elements. But it can be used much more flexibly by considering the relationship between the elements. For example, you may decide that the argument in one essay is well structured but your assessment of the language used is not so good. If these considerations include three or even more elements, you are moving towards an ever more thorough evaluation and one which is likely to prove more instructive as a guide for your own essay writing.

Survey

Read through the available essays. Take a comprehensive view of them. Consider each one as a whole avoiding any temptation to engage with the detail. Does the text flow, one point leading on to another in a smooth way with the visual images nicely integrated? Or, is it erratic, stopping and starting rather than moving forward with a sustained momentum, the visual images appearing like afterthoughts? Whatever answers are prompted by these questions they will help you decide whether the essays are well presented or not. Should you decide that one or more is well presented, you will want to know how this has been achieved if you are to benefit from their example. So, you will have to probe more deeply, ask more questions and then evaluate what you discover. Give yourself sufficient time to do this: it will very likely be time well spent.

Explore

Ask yourself, how is the essay structured? Does it follow the classic pattern of thesis, antithesis and synthesis, the three parts framed by an introduction and conclusion? If so, do each of the separate parts break down into several subsidiary sections perhaps indicating greater complexity? If the essay does not follow this classic pattern, how else is it structured? Does it begin promptly by reviewing a representative range of differing approaches and interpretations of the subject? Does it then evaluate these before moving on to a full statement of the author's point of view? Or, does it reverse this second structure, stating the author's position then comparing this with alternative ones? Given the important requirement to develop a strong argument, it is worth examining the section of an essay that most focuses on this: the central section in the classic pattern.

1

The academic essay is the most common written assignment for students of visual culture.

2

Whatever the brief, examine it closely to discover what are the implicit as well as explicit requirements.

3

There is no single way of writing an essay but there are standard requirements.

4

An academic essay requires a clear structure and well-developed, properly supported argument.

5

Most successful essay structures are fundamentally three-part ones; thesis, antithesis and synthesis.

6

When doing research, use your own words.

7

Use standard English and an agreed referencing system in an academic essay.

8

Do not use words or concepts you do not properly understand. Check their meanings first.

9

Ensure that the main text, quotations and visual images form a coherent whole.

10

Every element in an essay should be fully integrated into the final text.

06 Other written texts

Other written texts

139

**A small selection
of my 100 collages
Lloyd Smith, 2006**

This example of reflective writing not only explains how the journal was used but provides such an extensive catalogue of what it was used for that it has considerable claim to be representative of those by a majority of students. 'My journal entries are dated but don't cover every day – just what seems significant.... They include thoughts about particular projects, other people's criticism of my work, records of work we've been doing, planning notes, and even impressions of exhibitions....'

06 Other written texts

Self-reflective texts

Probably the most common activity for students of art and design practice is thinking in words about visible artefacts and visual experience in general. Much of this activity remains entirely private: reflexive thinking that is neither spoken aloud nor written down. But, on occasions the substance of these uncensored, reflexive thoughts finds its way into the more considered, deliberate language of spoken or written statements. Written reflections on why a particular specialist subject was chosen for undergraduate studies; statements made to accompany the display of art and design work; reflective journals or summaries of these, are all examples of students' verbalising their thoughts, feelings and experiences. More formal examples include writing a report, usually on a recently completed work placement or internment, and a critical review, usually of a current exhibition.

Expectations

As with the written essay, there is no universally correct way of presenting any of these other texts, but each one has become associated with certain expectations. An artist's or designer's statement made to accompany a display of their work is generally expected to offer some explanation, some kind of key that will open up the hidden meaning of the ambiguous imagery. But this is not always the case. A report is expected to be an objective, factual account, written in the most literal language, yet most are written from personal experience: an inevitably subjective point of view that is often difficult to reconcile with the expected objectivity. Self-reflective statements and journals are axiomatically personal, frequently employing a wide range of language, formal and informal, literal and literary.

In several important ways, the critical review formalises much of this diversity. The average reader of a popular newspaper expects the reviewer to provide the factual, denotative information necessary to any proper understanding of an exhibition. They expect the writer to give an interpretation of the exhibition as well as estimate how successful it is. It follows that any critical review is likely to be diverse in its approach, the descriptive, analytical and evaluative occurring in a single short paragraph, and eclectic in its use of language, the literal, metaphorical and rhetorical adopted as required.

140
Girl with books
Kate Bellamy, 2005

Faced with the question, 'Why did you choose graphic design?' this student's reply typifies that of many. 'I…am pleased when others understand my work and I communicate a message.'

A key factor in all these contexts is the audience. Like a diary, a self-reflective journal is written for the writer's personal use. Whatever language is meaningful to the writer, formal, informal, even slang, is acceptable. A report is always written for a specific audience and the language used should be appropriate to their needs and understanding. A single reading should be sufficient to understand the information. Critical reviews addressed to a wide audience should also be easily understood but the varied requirements presuppose a greater flexibility in the choice of language. Matching language and purpose is an important decision.

141

Some of my work on display
Lloyd Smith, 2005–6

Cataloguing the variety of experiences that might be included in a reflective journal, this student is representative of many. 'Unravelling the secrets of the golden rectangle, creating 100 collages and taking part in a live art installation are just some of the things I'm able to look back on.'

142a

onedotzero team

142b

Phillip from State
James Medcraft, 2005–6

This brief statement summarises the many surprises that can occur on student work experience. One of the revelations of being on a work placement is to learn that design agencies are not always what they seem. 'I found that "onedotzero"… does not actually design, this is left to State, the company who share offices with onedotzero.'

Choosing the subject to study

For students of visual culture, answering the question why they voluntarily chose their subject of study is one of the earliest occasions when they might be required to make a conscious, verbal statement about their engagement with their preferred specialist area. This is likely to happen first on the occasion of being interviewed for a course of study but it might, as in the examples quoted here, be one of the earliest written statements they are expected to make after they enter the course. All students, from whatever cultural and social backgrounds, will have already engaged with the inseparable links between words and visual images: this is part of everybody's experience. In the context of the visual arts, words are used to verbalise this visual experience, but within the literary arts, words are used to describe or create visual experience.

Exactly why anyone chooses to study or work within visual culture is as problematic as why they might have chosen to study and work in an entirely different, specialist subject. Narrowing down the specific area of choice does not reduce the problem of verbalising whatever is chosen. Our concern here is with the way anyone explains their preference. How does the language used make this clear? Given the variety of possible explanations there is a correspondingly large number of possible examples but, perhaps, these can be reduced to just three types of response: fundamentally subjective, less personalised, and very nearly objective. The rare exceptions are those where design itself is made out to be both an attractive and essential course of study for anyone. The language used, especially where written, will identify which.

As we have already noted, expressing a highly subjective point of view can be verbalised. There are many available examples from art and design history, theory and criticism, even more from the wider literary culture, whatever the language culture, but there is always the problem that the kind of language used might itself be too restrictive, too limiting in its vocabulary and connotative aspects to be properly intelligible to a wider audience. Within a particular, highly cultivated literary context, all kinds of literary devices, allusions and references are acceptable. This is not so within the context of a group of students from very diverse backgrounds without this readily available knowledge. It is not always the case within a group of students from the same cultural context either.

143

Why I chose graphic design
Kattya Denise Evia-Gomez, 2005

'Since I was a little girl I loved drawing. I would draw everywhere.... Everyone thought it was strange as my entire family are in the army or are engineers...but they believed I would change.'

This statement is fairly typical of why students choose the visual arts. It explicitly speaks of a persistent need to draw, the developing awareness of difference, of being other than the person her family expected, yet implicitly revealing that the need to draw did not pass. This is personalised reflection on why someone chose to study art and design. It is subjective in its approach and choice of language ('I', 'my entire family'), and particularly: 'Come inside and find out how it feels to be caught into the design world!'

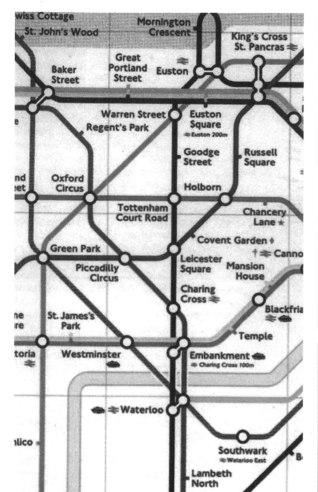

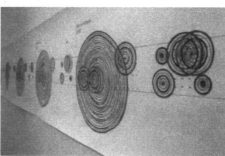

Far left: London Underground map
Left: experimental information design for Bakerloo line
Reiko Kasamo, 2005

A more objective study of choice is this one. 'I am interested in the functions of graphic design,' listing these as to identify, to inform and instruct, and to present and promote. The statement then becomes more particular, 'Specifically, I have a great interest in the second function; inform and instruct. I think the organisation and presentation of information is one of the most important but least recognised aspects of design. Information design such as road sign, product labels, operational manual are not spotlighted, yet it is essential to our life.' Again, the necessary 'I' in a statement of choice refers the thinking back to the writer but what is thought is given a wider social context. Reflective reasoning also helps explain the writer's interest in information design. 'I had majored business and commerce at university in Japan. Thereafter I worked in personnel management at a major rail company for five years. I acquired the skill of analysing information theoretically through these experiences.'

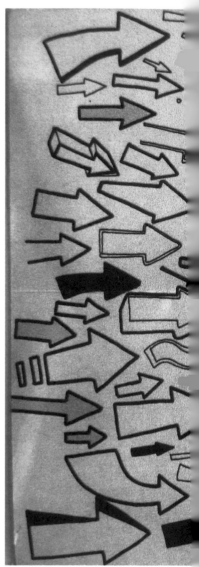

Why I chose graphic design
Jamie Howlett, 2005

The following quotation is the most direct statement of the reasons for choosing to study graphic design, matching a pair of objective explanations with a pair of more subjective preferences, all supporting the student's choice. 'Graphic design helps to make the busy world around us easier to understand.... The power of graphic design enables a simple circle to become a face with the addition of three extra pencil marks for a mouth and two eyes.... I chose graphic design...because of the interest I have with the world in which I live.... I like the problem solving process of graphic design and the way in which it challenges me.'

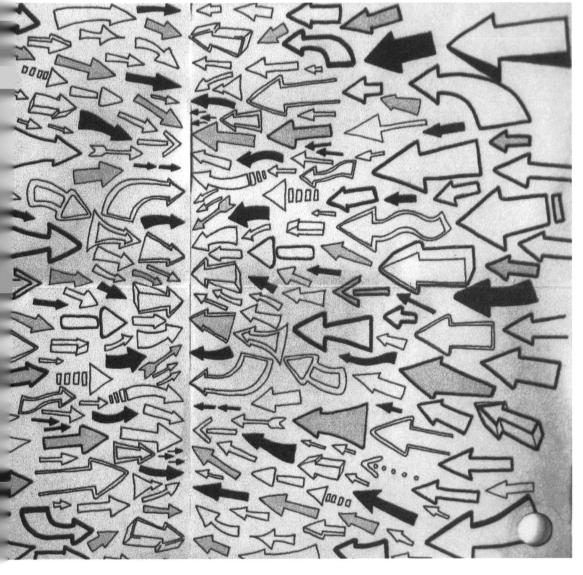

Directions (Arrows)
Greg Pearman, 2005

A more ruminated approach is exemplified in the following statement, one that repeatedly reflects upon aspects of graphic design but always to arrive at a confirmation of the choice of subject to study. 'I have always questioned my environment. It has made me to be an ideas factory…. We are still learning through visual images, our mind is like a child's, a sponge – soaking up all the new information, but most take it for granted and ignore the life passing before them. As a designer I embrace it.' Although the use of 'I' returns all the reflections back to the writer, the reflected thoughts refer to the collective experience ('our minds') of visual images. And this wider social awareness is confirmed later with, 'My work is concept driven. I make it challenging not only as a learning method for me but to allow the viewer to experience something themselves, not just be told…. I love what I do!'

The reflective journal

It is sometimes claimed that we remember better what we write down than what we read or hear. Making notes, recording responses, thoughts, feelings or creative ideas are effective ways of learning. The act of verbalising in itself places our reflections in the public domain of language. Writing these reflections down helps objectify our reflections. It provides some distance between the actual experiences and our recording of them. Language is never a private matter not even when we are silently fantasising. It is a collective experience and always pre-supposes an audience. Even the least analytical, reflective journal offers some proof of this.

Reflective journals can serve many purposes: they can be straightforward records of the facts of experience; accounts of where and under what conditions these were experienced; responses to these experiences; analyses of these experiences; or evaluations of these experiences. The thoughts and feelings can be of an immediate, even superficial kind or long pondered and probing. They almost always help clarify the experiences according to particular needs. For practising students of the visual arts, the reflective journal is most likely to address matters relevant to the subject and of particular concern, whether of a very practical nature or of a more personal, psychological kind.

147

Reflecting figure
Emily Franklin, 2006

The important role played by writing in the creative process is frequently recognised in these reflective journals. 'An interesting point about writing this journal was that it has made my work and thought processes ten times better than at the beginning of the year. In general, I'm quick at analysing a situation and knowing what needs to be done to make it work, but, when I recorded those thoughts on paper, I could see where I was not covering the whole ground and so could then broaden my way of analysing and thinking about things.'

Because a great deal of our thinking about visual culture is verbal (talking to ourselves but still in words), the reflective journal is likely to use the kind of language we use in ordinary conversation: it will be colloquial. If the journal is a set assignment, students should be cautious about using the specialist vocabulary and concepts particular to a subcultural group. The reader, especially the tutor assessing the journal, may not be familiar with this kind of language. Some use of the specialist language of visual culture is appropriate but this needs careful consideration. Successful communication requires consideration of the known audience.

148

Watching the sky
Giulio Miglietta, 2006

'I decided to give up my life lost in apathy to come to London…started to rent a small little room, working three days and going to school for four,' is a reflective journal entry that epitomises the experiences of so many students whether they are in London, Berlin, Tokyo, New York or anywhere else. But in the same journal is this much more reflective entry. 'When I was a kid, sometimes I used to spend time with friends watching the sky. Seeing bears, cars, people…in the cloud's shape…But, why do we feel different now? Why do we…feel really embarrassed when we try to act the same way?' This highly visual entry echoes Leonardo da Vinci's influential observation that stains and blotches on weathered walls contained suggestive images that could be the starting point for a picture; a practice later taken up by several Surrealists. But the entry as a whole suggests the child is locked up in the adult, struggling to get out. 'By the time we grow up we struggle with society to find our place in it. We are not the same as we were.' This is language rich in metaphor and the highly connotative.

149

Book project
Lloyd Smith, 2006

'My journal…acts not just as a record of all the assignments I have tackled and how I went about them, but also how I felt at the time…. Writing things down provides a marker of events that you can come back to later and perhaps helps filter experiences so you only write down what actually matters…. Having started the course with the idea of going into magazine design, it has been interesting to find myself undertaking a wide variety of projects that have made me look at alternative avenues…. I sometimes include a sketch in my journal or stick in the odd souvenir…it can be useful to jot down ideas in any spare moment. It worked well for the book covers, the most enjoyable project for me.' The language here is even more conclusive: reflecting back on recorded experiences then analysing them is a learning process in itself.

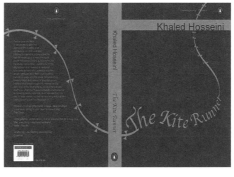

The Reflective Statement

Self-reflective statements by artists and designers can be found in a variety of contexts. An interview is one obvious example, the exhibition catalogue is another. But anyone who regularly visits exhibitions of art and design will be familiar with the widespread practice of displaying exhibitors' statements alongside the selected works. This is very often the case in group exhibitions where each contributor shows just a handful of items and is common practice in similar displays of student work. Giving a specific title to a piece already influences how viewers interpret the artefact. Adding a statement by the artist or designer, if only a short paragraph, will be even more influential in the interpretation of the work on show. The practice raises a number of significant questions.

If we accept the premise that language is not transparent, that whatever anyone says or writes has no fixed meaning, and that meaning ultimately rests in the interpretations of the listener or reader, the statements of artists and designers are as subject to this ambiguity as any other person's. If the creative work matches the stated intentions we might believe what the creator says but any disparity will raise doubts. If the final work is intelligible and worthy on its own terms but appears unrelated to the stated intentions, the doubts will increase. Statements by artists and designers need to be scrutinised before they are used and their possible effects carefully considered.

The use of verbal statements of any kind raises questions about the autonomy of any artefact of visual culture. When someone voluntarily puts words between the viewer and the work, they run the risk of being thought unsure about the work's ability to convey the intended meaning or, worse still, trying to determine how it will be interpreted. They may, however, be tacitly accepting that words and visual images are inseparably bonded and equally so in both contexts. Our everyday language betrays this interactive relationship. We *review*, carry out *revisions* and *envisage* outcomes. We *see* what someone means and have *insight* into their motives. Our reflections on the visual are largely conducted in words, but often with words that reflect the visual.

150

The nine colours of the soul
Federico de Cicco, 2005

This student's statement was brief, telling us little more than he had received a gift of 'a box of artistic brushes,' that he 'loved the person that gave it to me…my sister', and 'feeling the different sensations', of the brushes, 'I started to appreciate their value.' The statement concludes with the demand that we look at the painting to, 'find my real feeling'. Unlike the third example, no commentary or interpretation is offered. Yet, even here there is the implicit invitation to discover in the painted image some expression of the student's love for his sister. Despite all the arguments to the contrary, the authorial voice is still influential.

The value of Christmas
Disa Braunerhielm, 2005

This example mixes together factual information about the sums of money and a lottery ticket received as Christmas presents from four members of the student's family with the student's responses and revealing observations on each member. Exhibited together, the statement cannot be dissociated from the visual artefact, but however relevant the information might be, it offers no obvious explanation or commentary. The viewer must discover what links there are between, 'the sum is very generous', 'Money is always hard to deal with, especially as gifts,' '(Mum) thinks it's better and easier giving us money,' 'Dad doesn't like giving away money,' '(Granny) isn't able to go Christmas shopping,' 'The lottery ticket is both a joke and a tradition of the family,' and the very conceptual artwork on the wall.

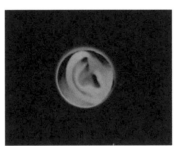

Underground project,
eye, ear, mouth and fingers
Federico Devoto, 2005

These four images appeared with a short statement by the student in a framed box much as in an exhibition but in this instance they appeared in the Explorative Study essay discussed in Chapter 5 (see page 150).

The display is preceded by the introductory sentence, 'I now would like to explain my work in order to delineate the influence (Odilon) Redon had on me during the development of the "Going Underground" project,' obviously seeking to contextualise the sources used in the final piece.

Anyone able to recall Redon's black-and-white lithographs of floating eyeballs can easily make the association with the cauterised imagery and comparably grainy texture of these monochrome photographs. The very evocative statement with its numerous adjectives lets us know what the artist meant to convey and why he chose the circular format:

'This series of images represents my real feelings about the underground, in particular when it is hot, busy and overcrowded, so macabre, darkness, claustrophobia were my key words.'

153

**Sky News studio
James Medcraft, 2005**

Reporting on the succession of work placements, this student recorded their dissimilarities ('Going from onedotzero (design agency) to Sky couldn't have been more of a contrast') and their similarities ('I soon found out that work for broadcast is not so very different as work for small design studios apart from the outcome of the work') but recognised some difficulties ('I had to learn a great deal of technical knowledge that week about how to design for broadcast at a professional level').

Written reports

The most important element in any report is the information it contains, and the degree to which the report is convincingly authoritative. To achieve this, the information should be accurate and clearly presented. The language used should be precise but easily accessible to the target audience. Above all, the information should be reliable. Anything that raises doubts in the reader's mind will undermine their trust.

A good report is much more than a well-ordered compilation of facts. Ordering the facts is interpretative, selecting them even more so. No report contains all the available information: deciding what is or is not to be included is the decision of the author. The general advice to be as objective as possible is not always as helpful as intended. A witness of events is part of the events, a participant even more so. Strict impartiality is impossible.

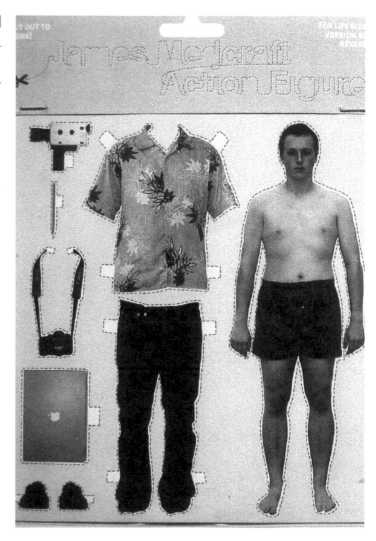

Action figure
James Medcraft, 2005–6

Faced with how to present himself
for consideration for internment or
a work placement, this student is
representative of many. 'I did not
have much time to prepare.... I
researched companies on the
internet and by looking through
Creative Review.... I had to assign a
style of work that represented me....
I decided...to create an Action-style
CV with a CD in the back which
contained a PDF of my work and a
Showreel.' This statement reports
on the earliest stages of the
internment process; the limitations
of time the search for possible
places and how best to present
himself and his work.

155

Image board
Amy Hyewon Lee, 2005–6

'One of the notions that scared me
the most was working to very tight
deadlines. They had a project for the
New York Fashion exhibition which
will travel around the world.... They
needed the image boards for each
area with different styling for the
presentation. I had a day to finish
the image boards for which I had
to use hundreds of images to
categorise into eight different areas.'
Specifically the student's
experiences and understanding, this
statement nevertheless maintains a
delicate balance between objective
reporting and subjective responses.

Internment reports

For many practising students of the visual arts, the most frequent requirement is to report on their relatively short work experience or much longer work placement or internment, sometimes lasting up to a whole academic year in industry. It is specifically the student's experiences and understanding that they are asked to write about even though their personal responses must be reconciled with verifiable circumstances and events. This is not always easily achieved, but it becomes easier with the recognition that not everyone reacts to or interprets the same circumstances and events in the same way, although their responses may be equally valid. Supporting evidence is required here, just as it is in the convincing argument of an academic essay.

It follows that writing this sort of report is different from, but not unrelated to, writing an essay or reviewing an exhibition. The all too easy similarities, however, can be a trap. When we read, our attention is directed by the text. The direction is decided, if not determined, by the author. The crucial factor is the relevant audience. To whom is the report addressed? What does the reader need to know? How should the material be organised? What kind of language should be used?

A student's work placement report is primarily addressed to their tutors. They will usually need to know how the placement was secured; be given a profile of the company or organisation and what it does; the role played by the student; what were the student's experiences and how they evaluated these. The tutors might also ask for recommendations that could be beneficial to other students taking up a place with the same company.

The most appropriate structure for the report is one that coherently organises the particular material. If the placement was with a single organisation the overall structure might be chronological or it might address the material from different but relevant aspects. If there were several placements with different companies these might still be dealt with chronologically but with each placement examined under the same subheadings. A concluding section might then make comparisons and critical evaluations. Whatever structure is used, well-chosen subsection headings, all properly listed in the table of contents, are useful indicators of what the report contains and where to find specific information.

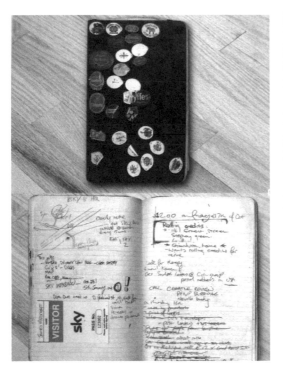

156
- -
Notebook/sketchbook
James Medcraft, 2005–6

'I had some good responses and advice from companies…which companies would be best for me and which people to contact…. I then started to go for interviews which led to my first placement.' These related note/sketchbook entries record interview dates, addresses and how to get there as well as things to be done. Following on from the same student's statement on the facing page (see fig, 154) the report at this stage continues the chronological progression of actions and events.

Language

The report's language should communicate as directly as possible. It should be literal rather than literary and avoid drawing attention to itself. A report is concerned with facts and communicating factual information even though it is interpreting and evaluating the facts. It is not the place for figures of speech, allusions, metaphorical images and rhetorical flourishes. Specialist, academic language or technical terms should be used only where necessary and only if the writer is confident that the target reader will readily understand. Abbreviations of company names (IBM), curriculum vitae (CV) and similar are acceptable providing a full spelling was given when the words were first used. Bullet points are also acceptable. They help keep the report as concise as possible.

A good report should be a lean document and athletics provides a suitable metaphor: the report should be as lithe and agile as a runner, carrying no unnecessary weight. This has little to do with the length of the report. It should be lean in the sense that it contains only necessary information. This information is best supplied in an equally lean, concentrated language. This can be difficult. Identifying a company's or organisation's profile can easily end up a tedious list if the writer does not carefully select the most distinguishing features and present these in a concise but engaging way. This is equally true of the often wide range of activities in which the student was engaged and in all such cases monotony must be avoided.

Some reports opt for a chronological, narrative approach, selecting key stages as in a storyboard and using these as a focus for profiling the company, contextualising the experience and identifying tasks undertaken. This structure can be effective but it must avoid being repetitious, either through the varied material available at each stage or the varied language employed to report on this material. Analysing the material relevant to each stage and aspect is, therefore, important if the report is to properly inform but avoid repetition.

Whatever the structure chosen for the report, the language should aspire to transparency, despite the many qualifications linguists might put upon this. The reader's attention should be directed towards the information being presented, not how that information is being presented. The language employed should pass unnoticed. For the writer of a report, this is a double-act. The writer must be acutely attentive to the language they use in order to ensure that the language does not impose itself between the reader and the information. There are parallels here with the familiar concept of art that conceals the artifice of the art. The outcome in both cases is something that appears natural and, therefore, convincing; real experience. But the more truthful reality is that the effect has been achieved by artifice.

**Marmalade studio
Pui Kwan Chan, 2005–06**

'Marmalade is an innovative magazine aimed at people in the creative industries…. It is a magazine that sets out to support fresh creative talent…[it] is a showcase of new talents in the creative industries: its target market is "culture influencers".' Almost a series of bullet points, this very nearly direct statement clearly identifies the company's profile with only a minimum number of connotative words, such as the choice of 'fresh' rather than 'new', or use of 'showcase' rather than 'presentation'.

**Lava is
Magali Nishimura, 2005–06**

'The main reason…was…to expand my awareness of design beyond the academic sphere…. Lava is a small Dutch agency based in Amsterdam…the first time I visited [the] Netherlands, I was overwhelmed by how attractive a simple tram ticket could be…. Everything, no matter how insignificant it might be, seemed to be meticulously designed…. Lava is non-hierarchical…. Every time a new designer comes or someone leaves, the company will change its character.' Three key factors in this report are clearly identified; the reason for undertaking a placement, the choice of location and the company profile. The statement is personalised, particularly in communicating an enthusiasm for Dutch design, but except for the emotive 'overwhelmed' the language is consistently matter-of-fact.

**T-shirt prints for Stylorouge
Magali Nishimura, 2005–06**

The wide range of roles played by any student is indicated in these statements, 'following an initial period of idleness and menial intern-type tasks I was given the opportunity to prove myself on a small project… working on the Planetarium project based in Saudi Arabia…a huge budgeted project…. My first design work was to come up with logos, designs and directional signage.' Overall, the reporting here is factual but although implicit rather than explicit, the student's response is evident in choosing 'menial' rather than 'ordinary', 'prove myself' 'rather than 'contribute to' and 'huge' rather than 'large'.

Barbican Art Gallery Level 3
Tropicalia
Win a holiday to Brazil
Visit www.barbican.org.uk/tropicalia

Wednesday 29 Mar 2006 £6.00 STU
Now open late until 9pm every night*

booking ref:

160

Entry ticket to Tropicalia exhibition

Professional art and design critics
with reviews to write for their
newspapers and magazines are
given free entry, press packs with
photographs of the exhibits and
often a catalogue without cost. They
are also paid for their review. A
student set an assignment to write a
critical review of an exhibition will
be given none of these and must pay
the entry price, albeit at a
concessionary rate. They will receive
no payment for their review. Do
these contrasted experiences
influence the writing of a review? Is
a student's response to an
exhibition very different from the
professional critic's?

Critical reviews

In his *Salon de* 1846, Charles Baudelaire, perhaps the greatest Western, 19th century critic of the visual arts, famously wrote, 'To be just, that is to say, to justify its existence, criticism should be partial, passionate and political, that is to say, written from an exclusive point of view, but a point of view that opens up the widest horizons.' His advice has been highly influential.

Requirements

In more contemporary terms, Baudelaire's statement encourages the critic to increase the reader's awareness, provide an appropriate cultural context but, above all, acknowledge subjective response, personal enthusiasm and a particular point of view. These are the most familiar characteristics of present-day art criticism. To write a review now is to engage with these issues whether you are a professional critic or a student.

Just as the majority of Baudelaire's mid-19th century readers were non-specialists, so are those today who read exhibition reviews. A relatively safe assumption is that most readers need to be informed about the subject of the exhibition, its historical and cultural context and what relevance it might have for us. This involves explanation and evaluation. It is an equally safe assumption that in general, reading reviews precedes visiting the exhibition. The reader, therefore, will need some indication of what the exhibition contains, how the exhibits are displayed and what supporting information is readily available. This involves description, interpretation and evaluation.

Language

Given that newspaper and magazine reviews, just as student reviews, rarely amount to more than a few hundred words and include only one, or at best two or three visual images, an ability to recreate the sensory experience of the exhibition can be as beneficial to the reader as any detailed analysis of items on show. It is within these constraints that literary skills in simile, metaphor, connotation and rhetoric become both desirable and necessary. Using an effective word or phrase can trigger a complex network of associative meaning that would require paragraphs to spell out in literal terms. For example:

'A special room is dedicated to Moholy's Light Space Modulator (1922–30). The structure made of mirrors, lamps, abstract shapes seems to live in several dimensions simultaneously. It sparkles, reflects, rotates, casts deep shadows and makes noise.'

If reading reviews precedes seeing an exhibition, the ultimate question the reader wants answering is: 'Is it any good?' Reviews, however, rarely offer a blunt yes or no. Approval and disapproval can appear in the same piece, the same paragraph and even the same sentence. Evaluative judgements are often dispersed throughout the review, sometimes no more than a clause or even phrase in a single sentence. They are sometimes implicit rather than explicit. All are acceptable practices. Describing, interpreting and evaluating are overlapping activities for most of us.

On occasions, the approach is interrogative, asking why something is so in the apparent absence of an appropriate answer, as in 'Why Albers and Moholy-Nagy?' This is a legitimate question. 'Linking these two men together with no other specific reason than their link to [the] Bauhaus,' is a valid point. As is the issue of balance between serious political matters and entertainment here. 'There is a dichotomy in the message presented and it is possible for a more "serious" message to get lost in the vibrant colours and sensory experience [of Tropicalia].'

The problem in any review is that it will prove to be too rhetorical, too 'partial, passionate and political' for the supporting evidence provided. If the review fails to match what it claims with what is identifiably shown in the exhibition it will be unconvincing. When this happens, the reader becomes disengaged, even disbelieving. Whatever trust existed at the outset of the review is lost. Writing a successful review requires considerable literary skill if the convictions of the reviewer are to be accepted by the reader.

161

Tropicalia exhibition poster

'The historical and social context of the body of work of the exhibition stems from the counter culture movement (Tropicalia), which emerged around 1967 as a reaction to the oppressive military regime in Brazil, which was set against the backdrop of Civil Rights marches and anti-Vietnam protest rallies in the US. There was a desire for the real "voice" of Brazil to be seen and heard across the board of popular culture in art, film and music etc. Tropicalia was born out of a desire to forge a new Brazilian identity out of the synthesis of dominant foreign culture, traditional culture and Modernism.'

After reading so informative and affecting an introduction as this, the reader will surely want to know how any of this material is made visible in the respective exhibitions. What artefacts are shown? Are they representative? How are they presented? What supporting information is provided?

162

Tropicalia exhibition exhibits

Generally, reviewers gravitate towards one or the other of two contrasting approaches, as in the next two quotations from student reviews of the Tropicalia exhibition. There is the factual report. 'The exhibition is split over two levels, and while the lower space is dominated by the interactive and installation pieces, with the scale and sounds almost overwhelming, the upper space is more contained with clearly divided sections and is more subdued.' Or there is the experiential one. 'At the core of the movement is the notion that art should be approached not with your intellect but first and foremost with your senses wide open…. Visitors are thrown into a multi-sensory experience – they walk bare-foot through a surreal shanty-town surrounded by a sandy beach…two screeching parrots and tropical plants gesture towards the exotic, heightening the effect of this sensory world.'

**Albers & Moholy-Nagy
Exhibition Poster**

This exhibition poster visually
paraphrases the rationalist,
geometrical and structural
characteristics promoted by
Modernist artists, designers,
theorists and critics. Characteristics
that were made particular in the
displayed work of Albers and
Moholy-Nagy. But for the critic of
the exhibition, the evocative
description of single artefacts is
most effective if they have already
been situated in a historical and
cultural context. This highly
concentrated paragraph does just
that:

'*Albers and Moholy-Nagy: From the
Bauhaus to the New World* is an epic
union of the work of pioneering
Bauhaus artists and teachers Lázló
Moholy-Nagy and Josef Albers.
The extensive exhibition compares
and contrasts the two artists' work
from some of their earliest to that
at the end of their careers,
exploring the transitions that they
both experienced, which were,
although not always consciously
overlapping, often the same. One
such example being their
emigration to America following the
closure of the Bauhaus in 1933 after
the Nazi's rise to power.'

The paragraph describes, analyses
and evaluates as it informs.

Light-Space Modulator
Lázló Moholy-Nagy, 1922–1930

Upward
Josef Albers, c.1926

All the following questions are addressed in this review of the Moholy-Nagy/Albers exhibition. How is the curatorial intention made visible? What artefacts are shown? Are they representative? How are they presented? What supporting information is provided? 'The exhibition is curated very carefully to create a "dialogue between two distinct…approaches to a common ideological ground"…with the audience's focus switching to and fro between artists as they move from one room to another. A sense of context or dialogue is never lost…. A loose chronology and adequate signage in each room gives a wider social and historical context to the work.' Modernist ideology is manifest in Moholy-Nagy's multi-functional structure (top); a mechanised, kinetic sculpture as well as device for light projection onto a screen or stage set. The same ideology is evident in the asymmetrical, orthogonal, flattened composition of Albers' picture (bottom).

Sampling three

How often do you read a piece of writing and, during the reading, pay as much attention to the text as writing (words on a page) as what you think these words mean? Are the occasions few or many? Your answers could be instructive. Writing, like painting or photography, is a medium: it mediates. The medium comes between what is mediated and how the subject is understood. It is, in itself, interpretative. If you wish to improve your performance (and performance it is) in either writing or speaking you must be attentive to the medium used and its effects.

In his work S/Z, (Editions du Seuil, 1970), Roland Barthes sets the conventionally readable (*lisible*) text against the writable (*scriptable*) one. The former kind of writing avoids drawing attention to itself: it appears transparent like a pane of glass in a window, we are expected to see through the medium to what is being mediated. The latter acknowledges the medium as mediator: the mediation draws attention to itself, demands an interactive response from the reader not a passive one. These are two very different kinds of writing and our awareness of the differences is relevant to our purpose here.

It is now much easier to understand why some kinds of writing carry an easier conviction than others. Mythologised speech, as Barthes has explained, appears natural, as in, 'Dad doesn't like giving away money'. This is matter-of-fact writing. Who would doubt it? But it can be deceptive. The avoidance of any rhetorical devices such as similes, metaphors and the connotative does not prevent it being as much of a cultural construct as any other verbal statement. The statement is still mediated through language with all its limitations.

Reading through the diverse examples of several different kinds of writing in this chapter or any other, do you still believe that language can be transparent? Are you now better able to distinguish between the different kinds of writing and the devices these employ? Have you discovered ways in which you might improve your own use of language in the context of visual culture? Do you feel more confident about verbalising the visual?

Purpose

For both writer and reader, identifying the purpose of a text is fundamental. What function should it serve? What is its subject? To whom is it addressed? Is the text accessible to the target reader? For the writer, these are basics determining everything from the point of view adopted, how the material used will be structured and the kind or kinds of language employed. For the reader, the writer's decisions must be persuasive. The text should minimise any possible doubts. A good test of any example of text is to ask how well the means employed fulfils its purpose. Are these well matched? There are no reliable rules for deciding beyond the generalised advice that the evidence supplied should be convincing. What is convincing to one reader may not be to another. There is no way of avoiding differences of intention or response, dependent as these are on a diversity of social and cultural factors.

Representation

Presentation or representation? We must be alert to the distinction. The former requires that we show something directly to another person or persons. This is easily understood if we think of the studio context where actual artefacts are presented for consideration. The latter is very different. It is an act of translation. To represent something involves mediation in order to bring to mind or into the imagination of another person or persons something which is not materially present. All visual images are of this kind. When we verbalise the visual, we are engaged in this act of translation. We are using verbal language to describe, analyse, interpret or evaluate what is presented in a visual language. Scrutinising the language used to do this is an invaluable experience. When you next read a text that successfully verbalises the visual, consider how this was achieved. What kind or kinds of language are used? What makes the language effective?

Context

Nothing exists in a cultural vacuum. Everything is produced and consumed within a specific social and historical context. The mathematical equation that 2+2=4 might be thought to transcend these conditioning factors but the choice here of Arabic rather than Roman numerals opens up a complex network of associated meanings. Whenever we verbalise the visual, we are engaged with these culturally conditioning factors. If, as author, we do not properly and adequately provide a context for the general subject or specific artefact in a text, much of what we write may be thrown into doubt. Ask yourself how often your understanding has been limited by a lack of contextual information. Was this a limitation of the author or, was it your limitation? If the book made clear its subject and level of address, were you up to it? Does this awareness make you more concerned to provide this basic information in your own writing?

Flexibility

The language best suited to writing a reflective journal is not necessarily suited to writing a report. There are distinctions between what is felt and what is understood. There are additional distinctions between what is a subjective response and an objective one. Each may be equally valid but they must be suited to the purpose and the context. Deciding what is best suited to the purpose and the context will help decide the appropriate language to be used. If you are seeking good models of practice, these considerations will help identify what is efficacious. If the intention in any writing about visual culture is to achieve a desired outcome, to be effective, then the written text must produce this effect: it should persuade the targeted reader. Flexibility is required. Are you sufficiently flexible to meet all the different written assignments set? Does your writing fall into habitual patterns or can you vary it according to need? The writer must be aware of the many alternative structures and kinds of language available. Familiarity with these differences requires reading a sufficiently varied set of texts. There are no limits to these.

Summary

1

Self-reflective thinking in words about visual experience is a regular activity.

2

Written statements of these reflections take different forms and are for different audiences.

3

The language used is equally varied but should be appropriate to the context.

4

Statements on their own work by artists and designers can inform and explain but they can misrepresent the autonomous visual artefact.

7

A written report is concerned with factual information and is for a target audience. The language used should be literal not literary.

10

Being specific is almost always preferable to generalising.

5

Self-reflective journals can be subjective and only for the writer.

8

A critical review balances factual information with a personal point of view but it should be written in standard English.

6

Always, the use of language assumes an audience. There is no private language.

9

Literary skills can be of great benefit in a critical review where the lack of any visual images put greater demand on verbalising the visual.

Conclusion

Conclusion

Effective speaking and writing about visual culture are vital skills for all students of art and design. An ability to verbalise the visual is as important in a casual conversation in the studio as it is in a formal, academic essay. Acquiring and improving these skills is an imperative.

The preceding chapters in this book have examined a wide range of contexts in which the need to verbalise visual experience is of great importance. In each case the spoken and written examples have been closely examined in order to discover what kind of language has been used and what made each example effective. Unravelling the examples is revealing and instructive.

An examination of language itself, how it works, what it can and cannot do, has been fundamental to the wider exploration of the uses of language and linguistic devices employed. Naming, describing, contextualising, analysing, interpreting and evaluating have shown themselves to be the core uses, with simile, metaphor, denotation and connotation the most frequently employed devices. On occasions, these became the means for measuring further examples. In turn, they could be used by the reader to explore other examples, including their own spoken and written practices.

Beyond the different uses of language it has become clear that there are different kinds of language. The basic vocabulary of standard English is greatly extended when we include the very specialised, but very different, language used in the contexts of academic art history, graffiti or any number of youth subcultures. From formal English (or any other language) to slang, the range is immense, but all these different kinds of language have their use. The greater our awareness of the many dimensions of a language the greater the possibilities available to us.

Taking advantage of this immense range requires identifying the distinctions that characterise these different kinds of language. This makes it easier to decide which kind of language to use in any particular context. What is appropriate for one purpose is not necessarily appropriate for another. Choosing the right kind of language is a major factor in any effective communication. Articulating the language clearly and confidently is another.

Learning by example is not only common practice in the visual arts; it is also common practice in language too. The many examples of spoken and written language offered here are just that. None is definitive. They are means to an end: improving the ability to use language successfully. It is for the reader to select what best suits their purpose.

The links between words and visual images are complex and indivisible. Making one effectively serve the other has been the central aim of this book.

Glossary

Alternative Culture
One or more cultures in opposition to the dominant one.

Appropriation
The selective practice of relocating some existing material into another thereby changing its meaning.

Avant-garde
Those in the forefront of innovative, progressive influences.

Binary
The system of opposites in which one side of the equation is prioritised over the other.

Burner
The graffiti equivalent for a masterpiece in academic, art-historical terms.

Canon
The catalogue of claimed masterpieces within a particular medium.

Counter-culture
Synonymous with alternative culture.

Deconstruction
A philosophical and theoretical position that identifies the multiple meanings available in a text, especially its internal contradictions.

Difference/Differance
Difference identifies what is specific to a person, thing or culture. Differance is a neologism coined by the Deconstructivist writer, Jacques Derrida, that conflates 'to differ' with 'to defer'.

Double Coding
The superimposition of one possible meaning upon another.

Ego
Pschoanalytical term for the determining the psychic force between the id and the superego

Ekphrasis
A literary description of, or commenting on, a work of art.

Free Association
A psychoanalytical method dependent upon the analyst's response to verbal and other material presented by the analysand.

Functionalism
A Modernist term identifying the fulfilment of the required needs.

Gaze
A term used to identify the relationship between the interested, motivated viewer and what is being presented, frequently associated with a genderised interest.

Getting Up
A graffiti term for writing.

Grand Tradition
The catalogue of claimed, exemplary masterpieces in a given cultural tradition.

Hybrid
Of mixed origin; heterogeneous.

Id
The psychoanalytical term for the source of all undifferentiated desires or fears.

Identity
A richly contested field that fundamentally pivots upon the nature versus culture argument.

Imperialism
The imposition of a dominant nation or culture's values upon those of a weaker one.

Intertextuality
The claim that all texts are written/created within a pre-existing network of texts that inform each other.

Masterpiece
Within the dominant culture a work that epitomises the highest claims of authority.

Mirror Stage
A psychoanalytical term identifying the moment of the child's recognition of its own reflection as being someone separate from its mother.

Meta-narrative
A Postmodern term identifying and rejecting any system of belief claiming universal application.

Modern
Of the present or recent times. A term related to modernity, identifying the condition of being modern, especially in its more progressive aspects, and Modernism, a highly selective set of ideas and practices: an ideology.

Oedipal Complex
A psychoanalytical term identifying the male fear of castration.

Other
A term used by cultural theorists in the context of identity to denote what is not self.

Patriarchal
Closely linked to the term 'phallocentric', both identify a male-dominated culture.

Performative
A term that emphasises the acting-out or role-play involved in the cultural structuring of identity.

Postmodern
An unresolved term indicating in its hyphenated form, post-modern, that which follows Modernism but embracing a far wider and more and more critical revision (see meta-narrative).

Scopophilia
The delight in looking.

Semiology/Semiotics
Synonymous terms for the study of signs, whether they be verbal, visual or other.

Sign
In semiology the sign is the combination of the signifier (the sound or its written equivalent of 'dog') and the signified ('dogness' or 'canine').

Superego
The psychoanalytical term for the internalised forces of cultural repression.

Superstructure
A Marxist term identifying the socio-cultural institutions and practices that both support and promote the interests of those who own the materials and means of production.

Symbolic Value
A Marxist term identifying the value we give to things that far exceeds their use value.

Synaesthesia
The overlapping of one sensory response with another as in 'hot colour'.

Tag
The adopted name or signature of a graffitist (or writer).

Throwup
The rapidly outlined signature of the graffitist.

Use Value
A Marxist term indicating the utilitarian value of something.

Picture credits

Picture credits

Introduction

01
Ham House Gardens, 1988
Sasa Marinkov. Courtesy and
copyright of the artist.

Chapter One

02
Image provided courtesy Peter
Freeman, Inc. New York.

06
*The Betrayal of Images/Ceci n'est pas
une pipe*, 1929, (oil on canvas). Rene
Magritte (1898–1967). Courtesy of
Los Angeles County Museum of Art,
CA, USA.

07
Courtesy of The New Art Centre,
Salisbury, Wiltshire, UK.

08
Courtesy and copyright of Ghaith
Abdul-Ahad.

09
Courtesy of the English Heritage
Photo Library.

10
Courtesy of Joseph Dirand
Architecture.
Photograph: Adrien Dirand.

13
Image courtesy and copyright
of the artist.

15
Musician, 1954-5, (purbeck freestone,
86 x 68 x 47cms). Mary Spencer
Watson. Courtesy of Stephanie Keil
and Julian Francis.

16
Courtesy and copyright of the artist.

17
Courtesy and copyright of the artist.

19
Courtesy of Blattner Brunner, Inc.
Pittsburgh, PA, USA.

20
Courtesy and copyright of the artist.

21
Reproduced with kind permission
of Unilever. (Client: Bertolli/Agency:
Cake/Photographer: Simon Paige
Richie/Creative Director: Mark
Whelan/Art Director: Simon
Moore/Senior designer: Jane
Tibhetts)

24
Courtyesy of Library of Congress
Prints and Photographs Division
Washington. Reproduction Number:
LC-USF342-T01-001167-A, (digital
file from b&w film dup. neg.), LC-
DIG-ppmsc-00231 (digital file
from print).

25
Courtesy of Apple Computer, Inc.

26
Courtesy of Miriam Rand.

Chapter Two

28
Courtesy of Michael Jones.

29
Virgin and Child with St. Anne, c.1510,
(oil on panel). Leonardo da Vinci
(1452–1519). Copyright Louvre, Paris,
France/Giraudon/The Bridgeman Art
Library.

30
Figure Study for Battle of Cascina, 1504,
(pen, brush, brown and grey ink).
Michelangelo Buonarroti
(1475–1564). Copyright British
Museum. London, UK/The
Bridgeman Art Library.

32
View of the façade, c.1566–67
(photo) by Andrea Palladio (1508–80)
& Vincenzo Scamozzi (1552–1616).
Copyright Villa Rotunda, Vicenza,
Italy.

33
Courtesy of the Martin Kamer
Collection.

38
Red and Blue Chair, c. 1918, (wood,
painted, height: 86.5 x 66 x 83.8 cm;
seat height: 33 cm), Gerrit Rietveld
(1888–1964). Courtesy of Museum
of Modern Art (MoMA), New York.
Gift of Philip Johnson. Copyright
2007, The Museum of Modern
Art/Scala, Florence.

40
Copyright Bildarchiv Foto Marburg.

42
Courtesy of Stapleton Collection.

43
Still Life with Bottle and Glass or
Le Vieux Marc, 1913, (paper cut-out,
wallpaper, newspaper and charcoal
on paper. Pablo Picasso (1881–1973).
Courtesy of Kunstsammlung
Nordrhein-Westfalen, Dusseldorf,
Germany.

44
Courtesy of Vitra Design Museum
Collection. Photographer Andreas
Sütter. Copyright Vitra
(www.vitra.com).

46
Photographer Ianthe Ruthven.

50
Impression no. 3 (Concert), 1911, (oil
on canvas). Wassily Kandinsky
(1866–1944). Courtesy of Stadtische
Galerie im Lenbachhaus, Munich,
Germany/ The Bridgeman Art
Library.

52
Copyright and courtesy of Albertina,
Vienna.

55a and 55b
Images courtesy of UNLV Library,
Special Collections.

57
Possession, 1976, (43 x 33 inches).
Victor Burgin. Courtesy and
copyright of the artist.

58
*Post-Partum Document, Documentation
IV: Pre-writing Alphabet, Exergue and
Diary*, (PPDVI), 1978, (resin and slate,
1 of 15 units 20 x 225.5cm each).
Mary Kelly. Courtesy Collection Arts
Council of Great Britain.

59
Untitled, 1983, (colour photograph 74
1/2 x 45 3/4 inches (MP# 122)). Cindy
Sherman. Courtesy of the Artist and
Metro Pictures.

60
Untitled, 1992, (silver print with
silkscreen. 38 x 26 inches. Edition of
5). David Wojnarowicz. Courtesy of
the estate of David Wojnarowicz
and P.P.O.W. Gallery, N.Y., USA.

64
Classical Ruins, late 17th century,
(oil on canvas). William Gowe
Ferguson (1632–95). Courtesy
Ham House, Surrey, UK. National
Trust Photographic Library/John
Hammond.

65
Courtesy and copyright of the artist.

66
Talking Presence, 1988, Sonia Boyce.
Courtesy of private collection.
Copyright the artist.

Chapter Three

68
Courtesy of Dyson Ltd.

75
Courtesy and copyright of the artist.

83
Mechanical Pig, 2005, (mechanical
sculpture; silicone, platinum /
fibreglass, metal, electrical
components, 40 x 58 x 62 inches).
Paul McCarthy. Courtesy of the artist
Hauser & Wirth Zurich London, UK.

84
Star Star, 2006, (acrylic and
styrofoam clown nose on canvas,
57 x 50 x 3.5 inches). Jason Fox.
Courtesy the artist and Alexandre
Pollazzon Ltd., London, UK.

87
Trilogy Part 2, 2006. Daniel Gustav
Cramer. Courtesy the artist and
Domobaal

88
The Twins, 2006, (marble and lead
82 11/16 x 46 7/8 inches). Gary
Hume Photograph: Stephen
White. Courtesy Jay Jopling/
White Cube (London, UK).

91
Courtesy and copyright of Sean
Elliott.

92
Guerrillero Heroico, 1960. Alexannder
Korda Copyright KORDA. All rights
reserved.

93
Courtesy archive 212Berlin.

94
Courtesy archive 212Berlin.

Chapter Five

122
Courtesy and copyright
of Adbusters.

126
Courtesy of the Collection Van
Abbemuseum, Eindhoven, the
Netherlands.

130
The Eiffel Tower, 1889, (panel).
Georges Pierre Seurat (1859–91).
Courtesy of Fine Arts Museums of
San Francisco, CA, USA.

131
Courtesy of Library of Congress
Prints and Photographs Division
Washington, Reproduction Number:
LC-USZ62-102634.

132
Bathers at Asnieres, 1884 (oil on
canvas). Georges Pierre Seurat
(1859–91). Copyright National
Gallery, London, UK/The Bridgeman
Art Library.

133
*Place de la Concorde (Viscount Lepic and
his Daughters Crossing the Place de la
Concorde)*, (oil on canvas, 78.4 x
117.5 cms). Edgar Degas. Copyright
The State Hermitage Museum, St.
Petersburg (Inv. No ZK-1399).

135
Courtesy Deutsche Kinemathek,
Berlin.
Photograph: Horst von Harbou.

136
La Citta Nuova, 1913, (ink, pencil and
watercolour on paper). Antonio
Sant'Elia. Courtesy of Private
Collection.

137
Copyright Bildarchiv Foto Marburg.

138
Staatliches Bauhaus, 1995, built
1925–26. Photograph, German
School (20th century), Dessau,
Germany.

Chapter Six

161
Rita Sylvester, 2003, (decal, master
digital file and certificate of
authenticity variable). Courtesy
of John Connelly Presents, New
York, USA.

162
Images taken from *Tropicalia A
revolution in Brazilian Culture* held at
Barbican Art Gallery 16 February–
21 May 2006. Courtesy of the
Barbican Art Gallery.

163
Courtesy of Tate, London 2007.

164a
*Light-Space modulator (Light requisite
for an electrical stage)*, 1922–1930
(reconstruction 1970), (chrome-
plated steel, aluminium, glass,
acrylic glass, wood). Lázló Moholy-
Nagy. Photograph: Bauhaus-Archiv
Berlin/Fotostudio Bartsch.
Copyright: VG Bild-Kunst Bonn.

164b
Upward, c.1926, (sandblasted flashed
glass with black paint, 171/2 x 12 3/8
inches). Josef Albers. Copyright
The Josef and Anni Albers
Foundation/Artists Rights Society,
New York/DACS, London, 2007.
Photograph: Tim Nighswander.

Page numbers in brackets
denote illustrations.

Acknowledgements

I would like to thank Caroline Walmsley, Lucy Bryan and Brian Morris at AVA Publishing whose commitment and support have seen me through some difficult moments; Malcolm Southward, designer, whose ingenuity can be seen on every page of this book; Sarah Jameson, picture researcher, for her resourcefulness; and Graham Goldwater, photographer, for his invaluable help with many of the pictures.

At the outset of the project I had very profitable conversations with Margot Blythman and Colin Davies, both of whom were very encouraging.

I would also like to thank Sasa Marinkov, Michael Jones and Sebastian Loew for allowing me to use their work as illustrations and Martin Kamer for allowing me to use work from his private collection.

Last but not least, I would like to thank the very many students who so generously and enthusiastically agreed to my using their spoken and written words and, in a substantial number of cases, their design work too. Without them, the book could not have been realised:

Keisha Ferrell, Sara Colding, Lakweena Suit, Alexis Mutkin, Matthew Rogers, Susan Gerrard, Olli Vainamo, Radka Schling, Ken Kirton, Charlie Armstrong, Fernando Ribeiro Rodrigues Junior, Martin Richardson, Joseph Owen, Patricia Cecilia Ofuono, Heylen Espinosa-Casallas, Sam Marriott, Peter Robertson, Kate Bellamy, Lloyd Smith, James Medcraft, Kattya Denisse Evia-Gomez, Reiko Kasamo, Jamie Howlett, Greg Pearman, Emily Franklin, Giulio Miglietta, Federico Devoto, Disa Braunerhielm, Federico de Cicco, Amy Hyewon Lee, Pui Kwan Chan, Magali Nishimura, Marina Bowater, George Hurst, Louise Matell and Laura Liebrecht.

Michael Clarke